Maud Howe Elliott

Atalanta in the South

A Romance

Maud Howe Elliott

Atalanta in the South
A Romance

ISBN/EAN: 9783744673471

Printed in Europe, USA, Canada, Australia, Japan

Cover: Foto ©Thomas Meinert / pixelio.de

More available books at **www.hansebooks.com**

ATALANTA IN THE SOUTH.

Atalanta in the South.

A Romance.

By MAUD HOWE,

AUTHOR OF "A NEWPORT AQUARELLE" AND "THE SAN
ROSARIO RANCH."

BOSTON:
ROBERTS BROTHERS.
1886.

University Press:
JOHN WILSON AND SON, CAMBRIDGE.

TO

THOSE DEAR SOUTHERN FRIENDS

Whose unfailing kindness and hospitality made the half year passed in New Orleans one of the pleasantest of my life, I dedicate this Romance in a loving and grateful remembrance.

Before the beginning of years
   There came to the making of man
Time with a gift of tears;
   Grief, with a glass that ran;

And the high gods took in hand
   Fire, and the falling of tears,
And a measure of sliding sand
   From under the feet of the years;
And wrought with weeping and laughter,
   And fashioned with`loathing and love,
With life before and after,
   And death beneath and above,
For a day and a night and a morrow,
   That his strength might endure for a span,
With travail and heavy sorrow,
   The holy spirit of man.

Eyesight and speech they wrought
   For the veils of the soul therein,
A time for labor and thought,
   A time to serve and to sin;
They gave him light in his ways,
   And love, and a space for delight,
And beauty, and length of days,
   And night, and sleep in the night.
His speech is a burning fire;
   With his lips he travaileth;
In his heart is a blind desire,
   In his eyes foreknowledge of death;
He weaves, and is clothed with derision;
   Sows, and he shall not reap;
His life is a watch or a vision
   Between a sleep and a sleep.

ATALANTA IN CALYDON: SWINBURNE.

ATALANTA IN THE SOUTH.

CHAPTER I.

THE time, a December afternoon within the
memory of a child of ten ; the place, Jackson
Square, better known to history as the old Place
d'Armes, the centre of all that is most interesting in the French quarter of New Orleans.

The bronze effigy of the hero whose name the
square now bears is surrounded by a group of
belated rose-bushes full of a sober wintry bloom.
Outside of these runs the shell-strewn path, daz-
zling white, and harsh to tread upon.   The flowers are all dead, save the hardy northern roses,
but the orange-trees are heavy with their golden
fruit.   A group of black-skinned children are
playing at leap-frog, and their young voices
sound cheerfully in the ears of Philip Rondelet
as he sits at the window of his modest apartment
high up in one of the famous Pontalba buildings.
Two sides of the square are flanked by long
brick houses of a somewhat imposing character,
alike in all particulars to the very monogram of

their owner, wrought in fine ironwork above the
central windows, where the façade rises to a high
peak. The lower floors are now occupied by
shops of a more or less unsavory aspect, for fashion, which once was at its height in Jackson
Square, has flown to a newer and less attractive
part of the city. Among the tenants of the fine
old Pontalba buildings there are few to-day who
claim any connection with polite society. Rondelet might have been classed with the excep-
tionals in this respect, as he should be in many
others. He certainly was exceptional in his appearance, and no less so in his tastes, if we may
judge by the glimpse we catch of him sitting in
his small study under the leads, staring dreamily
out into the square below. There were very few
articles of furniture in the room, and the floor
lacked a carpet. A third of the space, that part
where the sun lay longest, was devoted to a miniature garden, where the flowers bore all the marks
of a careful and loving hand. Rare and splendid
orchids hung from the wall, and a superb oriental
flower, looking like a vast vegetable butterfly,
bloomed serenely forth from the neck of a broken
wine-bottle. A row of Japanese dwarf-oaks
made a sombre background for a vivid staff of
Mexican cactus-flowers. In the midst of all
this tropical bloom stood a large aviary, where
a dozen birds twittered and trilled and dipped

their dainty wings in a tiny fountain playing in the centre of the cage. A bare deal table, a lounge which had lost its cover, a worn horse-hair armchair, and a set of unpainted pine shelves laden with books, completed the contents of the apartment, with one notable exception. On the mouldy, unpapered wall hung an un-framed picture representing the head and shoul-ders of a man. At the first glance it might have passed for an ancient copy or original study of a head of Christ. On closer examination it was seen to be only the portrait of a man whose feat-ures bore the stamp of the highest intellectual beauty, — a long, delicate face, with a broad, un-ruffled forehead, large eyes of that indefinable gray-blue tint which neither color describes, a thin, delicate nose, and a mouth of rare beauty and sensitiveness. The hair and beard, of a golden brown, fell about the shoulders, and below, folded upon the breast, were the white, nervous hands, with a delicate blue tracery of veins. If any one unsatisfied with this examination should have looked more closely at the picture, he would have been able to make out this inscription : "Philip Rondelet, from his friend Hans Makart." By the fading light of that short winter day let us look into the face of the man who is still gaz-ing out into the sunlight slowly waning from the square below. It is the same face as that in the picture; Hans Makart, friend to Philip Rondelet, having painted the man as he was, with that superficial resemblance to the Master which at a second glance was almost lost. The beauty, the gentleness, the love, are all there; but the power which raises these elements to achieve the salvation of man is lacking.

It is already dark on the stairway, though the last sunbeam is resting for a moment on the golden cross of the cathedral over the way. A sound of stumbling in the passage causes Rondelet to glance rather nervously towards the door. He is not in the mood for visitors, if we may judge from the impatient sigh which escapes him. The sound of voices in altercation reaches him, a silence follows, and from an inner door his black servant enters the apartment.

" Well, Hero ? "

" A gentleman to speak with you, sar."

" Say that I am not at home."

" I did, Marse Philip; but he says he knows yer are."

" Tell the gentleman that you have searched the extensive apartment, and that I positively am not to be found."

"Very good, sar."

Hero disappeared. Rondelet listened. There was the sound of a dispute, then a scuffle in the passage, a noise as of a person falling heavily against the wall, an exclamation in Hero's voice; and the door was thrown violently open, a stranger stood upon the threshold bowing civilly, hat in hand.

" Dr. Rondelet ? "

" Rondelet is my name, sir."

" I have forced myself into your presence, in spite of your servant's refusal of admittance, because I must speak with you on a matter of the utmost importance."

Rondelet bowed and remained silent. His visitor continued, —

" You are a physician ? "

" I have my degree as doctor of medicine, but I am not a practising physician."

" I was told that, Doctor, by Mr. Robert Feuardent, at whose instance I have come to ask your services in a matter of the strictest confidence."

The two men had remained standing. At the mention of Feuardent's name, Rondelet motioned his visitor to his solitary arm-chair and took his seat upon the coverless sofa.

" Feuardent assured us of your great skill, especially in a case of this description."

" Surgical? "

" Yes."

" A wound ? "

" It is feared a fatal one."

"It is an affair?—"

"Of honor."

"It would be wiser to seek some one of the established physicians here. I have not as yet undertaken any practice since my return from Paris. I am almost a stranger in my native city."

"It is for this reason that you would not be suspected of any connection with the affair, should it come out."

"There is danger, then, of a thorough investigation?"

"Possibly."

"I do not like the business. Besides, I don't see how I can go. I have an engagement at six o'clock which I cannot break."

"A dinner?"

"Yes."

"At Mrs. Darius Harden's?"

Rondelet looked somewhat annoyed at this cross-questioning, but nodded assent.

"Feuardent was to have been of the party. I am to carry his excuses. It is now half past five. At exactly a quarter past six I shall call for you at the Hardens'. A physician is always liable to be called away, and you will be absolved of all blame if you only put in an appearance at six."

The visitor rose, and Rondelet noticed for the

first time that he wore evening-dress. His linen was crushed and tumbled, and as he buttoned his over-coat closer across his breast, the doctor's eye caught a dark-red stain on the shirt.

" The affair took place this morning ? "

" Yes ; I drove out from the ball."

The man was going. Rondelet made a struggle to free himself from this mystery into which he was being forced against his will.

" Monsieur, neither you nor Robert Feuardent have the right to ask this thing of me. Your name I do not even know. I refuse to be accessory to this affair. You must have had some other practitioner upon the field."

" A mere boy, who has lost his nerve and insists upon a consultation with some one less unskilled and timid than himself."

Philip flushed, and his visitor, with a formal bow, vanished.

"Till a quarter past six," he called from the lower hall.

The two men had begun their conversation in English, but had quickly lapsed into French, after the manner of their kind under all strong excitements.

To these people, with whom the two languages are spoken indifferently from the cradle, the Latin tongue is the natural expression of all strong emotions.

Mechanically Rondelet changed his dress; and as he was about to go forth, he paused irresolute, unlocked a drawer beneath the bookshelves, and took out a case of surgical instruments. The dust was thick upon the box. He touched the spring, to make sure that everything was in its place; and at the sight of the shining steel the old repugnance came over him with stronger force than ever. He closed the box with a quick movement of disgust, and threw it back into the drawer. At that moment the stranger's words echoed in his ear: "Some one less timid than himself." That decided him. He slipped the instruments into the pocket of his over-coat and ran lightly down stairs into the street. It was very cold; the wind spitefully wrenched open the garments of the few people who were abroad, and rattled the great iron gates of the ancient court-house. It had come from the northern ice-fields, and gloried that the South could not rob it of all its fierce pain. Enough was left to pinch the faces of the poor folk, wretchedly housed for such weather, and to make the rich wish regretfully that their fire-places were more in accordance with Northern notions. At Mr. Darius Harden's comfortable house on Esplanade Street, however, there was little needed to complete the air of warmth and cheer.

The large drawing-room was lighted comfortably, though not brilliantly. The guests already assembled had drawn into a semicircle before the fire, and were listening to Mrs. Harden's last good story, when the door opened, and Philip Rondelet entered.

"Forgive me if I am late, kind hostess," he said; "and," he added, looking over Mrs. Harden's shoulder, "tell me, while she is not looking, who that young girl in white is. Do I know her?"

"No; it is Miss Margaret Ruysdale, a stranger from the North, — here for the winter with an invalid papa, the gentleman with one arm. I will present you to her, as you are to take her in to dinner. Miss Ruysdale, Mr. Philip Rondelet."

The young man made a deep obeisance, and the girl bowed simply to him, with nothing of the drooping of the lids or sudden uplooking into his eyes which he had often noticed in his introductions to young women in society. This Margaret Ruysdale from the North looked at him as quietly and civilly as she would have looked into the face of his grandmother.

"I have seen you before, Mr. — should I not say Dr. Rondelet?"

"I hardly know, mademoiselle; this is the second time to-day I have been so called. I *had* thought that I had left my title, along with my profession, on the other side."

"In Paris ; it was there I saw you."

"In Paris?" Rondelet smiled, his whole face lighting up with a look of unspeakable pleasure. It was as if a lover had suddenly heard the name of his absent mistress.

"Yes ; ah, how you miss it! I feel it in your voice," said Miss Ruysdale, her own voice growing, in sympathy, a trifle less like the murmur of cool running water than at first.

"Miss it? Ye gods, how I miss it! I suffer for it. Where did you see me? I never can have seen you ; I should not have forgotten your face."

"It was at the hospital, where I went once to make the portrait of a dying child for its mother. You took care of the little fellow André ; don't you remember him, — the son of your *concierge?*"

"To be sure, poor. little soul! How bravely he bore it all! It was better that he died; he could never have walked again. You, then, mademoiselle, are the young art student who paid —"

Miss Ruysdale interrupted him, —

"Yes, yes, I was his friend. How long is it since you left Paris?"

"A month, a year, a cycle, — I cannot say.

It seemed very long ago this morning ; but you have brought it back to me so vividly, it might have been yesterday. Have you neglected your profession as I have mine ? You were modelling in those days, were you not ? "

" Yes, I am a sculptor, and am always at work."

Looking down, Rondelet noticed that her small, bare hands, lying loosely clasped, were unusually firm-looking for those of so young a person. Margaret Ruysdale, sculptor, could hardly have more than attained her first score of years. He was ten years her senior, and since his last birthday had known the pain of finding himself no longer in the twenties. His feet were still hesitating what life-path to tread, and this slim girl quietly claimed the profession which had counted among its followers some of the greatest men the world has known. Her assertion had been made very simply and without assumption. She was a sculptor, and used as best she could the tools of Phidias and Angelo.

" I am to take you in to dinner," said Rondelet, as a general move was made in the direction of the dining-room.

" I am very glad," answered Margaret Ruysdale, sculptor, laying her small white hand upon his arm with the air of a comrade. She had put aside all coquetry, if she had ever possessed it,

2

which to Philip Rondelet seemed very doubtful ;
and yet nothing could be more feminine than her
face and figure, her well-modelled white gown
and appropriate ornaments of yellow gold.

"Tell me, is Mr. Robert Feuardent among
the guests? I heard I was to meet him to-
night."

Robert Feuardent! Rondelet started at the
name and glanced at the clock. It was nearly
half-past six. At that moment the door-bell
was violently rung, and immediately afterwards
a servant whispered a message in Mrs. Harden's
ear.

"Mr. Rondelet, a messenger has come for you,
summoning you to a sick person ; can you not
send him for some other physician?"

Philip set down untasted the glass of wine
he had raised to his lips, and said, "Tell the
person that it is not possible for me to leave
at present. He should summon another physician. Dr. N—— lives half a block from here."

In two minutes the man returned. "The
gentleman says, sir, that he can wait, but that
you will hardly like to keep a lady waiting in
the carriage on such a night as this."

"Mrs. Harden, you must excuse me. Mademoiselle, I cannot express to you my regrets at
being forced to lose the pleasure of knowing you
better."

"I am very sorry too; but of course your professional duties must take precedence of everything else. Good night, and god-speed to you," said Margaret Ruysdale, sculptor, with a smile, the first she had given him. Her smiles were not plentiful, and this one was to the unwilling Samaritan like a draught of the rich strong wine he had left untasted.

In the hall he found the young man, who was still a stranger to him, looking wan and pale beside the merry circle he had just quitted.

" You look ill yourself, my friend ; you are not fit to be out on such a night."

The stranger made an impatient gesture of dissent and threw open the door. A whiff of the chill north wind burst in at the opening, and fanned the flame in the chandelier, and blew into the face of the girl from the North, as if it bore her a greeting from her home. Outside, the street was empty and silent. A chill dense rain was beginning to fall, and the horses of the carriage which awaited them were fretting and tramping uneasily. " Get in as quickly as you can," said the stranger ; " there is one person on the back seat."

Rondelet placed himself beside the person on the back seat, the young man sprang into the carriage, and the horses leaped forward into a gallop. As his eyes became accustomed to the darkness, the young physician observed that the person beside him was a woman.

A lace scarf was thrown about her head and shoulders, bare, save for this slight protection, through which sparkled a profusion of jewels.

" Madame, have you no cloak ? "

There was no audible answer ; but the woman shook her head, indifferent alike to the cold and his solicitude. Rondelet wrapped her quietly in his own coat and leaned back in the carriage, absently watching the woman who sat beside him with hands closely locked and wild eyes staring out into the night.

CHAPTER II.

It was a relief to Philip Rondelet when the carriage stopped after a half hour's drive, before a small house of the meanest appearance. No matter what might lie before him, it could not be worse than that drive had been through the absolute darkness of the night with these two strange companions.

The young man had not spoken during the whole drive, and the woman, save for sudden bursts of passionate rage or grief, made no sound.

They were evidently expected at the hut, for the door was opened a few inches and a voice asked, " Has he come ? "

" Yes, yes, they are both here," answered the stranger. " Quick! let us in, for God's sake ; we have seen enough of this accursed night from outside." As he spoke, the young man pushed his way into the house, leaving the woman and Rondelet to follow him. They found themselves in a low bare room, where a fire burned smokily on the hearth.

"Where is he?" asked the woman in a low voice, speaking for the first time. She was, judging from her appearance, of Spanish extraction, and she spoke English with some hesitation.

"Above there," answered the man who had opened the door, a young physician whom Rondelet recognized as an acquaintance.

"I will go to him," said the woman, moving rapidly to the foot of the ladder leading to the loft.

"Stand back, will you? You can't see him till the doctors say 't will do no harm. Have n't you done him enough mischief already?"

The young man spoke roughly, almost brutally, to her, and pushed her from the ladder with no gentle hand. The woman sank on the floor before the fire without a word, and the young doctor led the way up the ladder after barricading the door firmly. He had taken the only light in the room, and Rondelet stopped for an instant to throw an armful of brush upon the dying fire. The woman thanked him with a mute gesture, and he followed the two men to the upper room. It was as desolate as the one he had just quitted. On a couch in the centre of the attic lay the man. On a table near the bed were surgical appliances, a roll of bandages, an ewer of water, and an empty pistol-case. On the floor, near the door lay a heap of torn clothing which seemed to have been cut from the body. Beside the patient crouched a huge mastiff, with one paw placed upon the bed. The creature's eyes were fixed on his master's livid face ; he acknowledged their entrance by a quick side glance, but never stirred from his post. The wounded man was a stranger to Rondelet ; the latter saw only that he was young, possibly twenty-four years of age, and proceeded to examine the wound. It was in the left breast, and a short examination showed that it was fatal; a few hours at most were all of life left to him. Gently replacing the bandages, Rondelet smoothed the pillow of the dying man and applied a strong restorative to his lips. In a few minutes the patient's eyes opened. He looked in Rondelet's face, and then said faintly, " You are the other doctor ? Best tell them it 's all up with me. I knew it from the first. Therese, is *she* here ? Jean, you promised."

His breath failed him ; the two physicians bent over him. In a moment he was easier.

" Is it true, Rondelet ? Tell me, is there no hope ? " It was Jean who spoke, in an undertone.

" Not the slightest ; it will soon be over."

" It cannot hurt him to see that she-devil downstairs ? "

" He is past hurting, poor fellow. If he wants
to see her — it is her name he just spoke ? "

" Yes."

" It can do no harm ; send the woman up."

" Mind you stay there, both of you ; do you
hear ? She is not to be trusted alone with him,"
said the man who had been called Jean, as he
left the room.

" Therese," groaned the sufferer.

She was beside him as he spoke her name, —
a splendid figure, thrilling with life and passionate love or anger, beautiful as a young tigress.

She fell upon her knees at the bedside ; and
lifting his helpless hand in both of hers, bathed
it with tears and kisses. Rondelet would have
left them alone together, but remembering the
warning, turned his face to the wall ; the younger
surgeon followed his example. But human sympathy was too strong for them ; a minute had not
passed before both men turned and gazed upon
those two figures, one so full of life, the other so
near to death. The woman was speaking rapidly in a low voice, and the man was lying with
closed eyes. He turned his face from hers and
sighed wearily.

" What does it matter to me now, Therese ?
One thing you must hear and understand, — *I*
was to blame. Do you hear ? It is my last word,
— I was to blame. The men will all tell you so ; I

forced him to fight against his will. He fired the
first time in the air. My pistol missed; then I
seemed to lose my senses, and ran toward him
shooting as I went. He fired once to save himself—"

The woman's loosened hair, black as the darkness into which he was drifting, hung about him;
she put her hand in his and carried it to his lips.
He pressed a faint kiss upon her pale fingers, and
then pushed the hand away; it was his last action. Consciousness then left him, never to return; and twenty minutes later the crystal mirror
held before his lips remained unclouded, the mass
of wild dark hair heaped upon his bosom was
unstirred by the faintest breath. All was over.
Since that mute gesture of avoidance, that
putting aside of her clinging hands, the woman
had not moved; not more still than she was the
dead form beside her. She had watched him
with untrembling eyelids, all intelligence had left
her face; it was as if her longing soul was clinging to the out-going spirit, even as her hands
clung to his helpless hands, which in the last
hour had pushed hers aside.

She might have striven to follow him on the
first stage of that dark journey, — in vain; for
the color came back to her marble cheek, the expression to her dark eyes. She leaned over him
as if to kiss his forehead for the last time; but the

jealous mastiff caught at her hand and bit the small fingers till the blood started. She did not seem to heed the pain, but the action was not lost upon her. With a faint moan she sank upon the floor, and lay there weeping and dishevelled, while the mastiff took up the note of grief with his low howl of pain.

Philip Rondelet, gentlest among men, took pity on this broken creature, whom the other men heeded as little as they did the dog, and got her finally into the lower room. She was passive in his hands, but sank again grovelling to the earth, her glorious hair falling about her, her rich dress and jewels lighting up the dark hovel. Soon the young surgeon and Jean followed them. The latter spoke to her less roughly than before, but with a scornful pity scarcely less hard to bear. At the sound of his voice the woman arose, silent and patient.

" Therese, you must go back to the city with the doctors. There is nothing more for either them or you to do. Launce and I will stay with him till they come to take him away. Remember, you are to know nothing of this till you hear the news from outside. It will be bad for you if you let fall anything that you have seen."

She nodded silently.

" For his sake," he went on, " it must never be known how and in what a cause he died.

His reputation is all that is left me to care for. Remember."

. "And the man who did this thing, is he to go unharmed?"

" He is wounded."

" Ah!" with a savage gleam of triumph; "but not seriously?"

"No, not seriously."

" But I swear — "

" Silence! The fault was yours, *yours, yours.* Do you hear? This man's blood is on your head, and his murderer's guilt upon your soul. Now go, and never let me see your accursed face again!"

With a gesture of supreme contempt he turned and left her. To Rondelet the young man said, " Good-by! I thank you for what you have done. He was my brother, my only friend—"

Rondelet wrung his outstretched hand. "Your name. Tell me that before I go?"

" No, it is better that you should not know it. I hope that you will hear no more of this affair."

" And the name of the man who killed him?"

" That I shall never tell."

The gray dawn was stealing on the sleeping world as Rondelet turned his face from the house of death. By the dim cold light he saw the double row of mighty moss-grown oaks, tongue-less witnesses of this and many another such an affair of honor. The shrouded trees drooped beneath the heavy, rain-soaked moss like so many forest giants clad in ashen winding-sheets. When he reached Jackson Square, the first sun-beams were fingering the gold cross over the way. What a night had passed since the last beam of the evening sun had fallen on the same spot!

The stairs were still dark; at the top of the first flight his foot encountered some slippery substance, and he fell heavily forward, putting out his arm to save himself.

When he reached his room he found that his left arm was badly sprained. He would have no use of it for several weeks, and would besides be obliged to wear it, for some days at least, in a sling. After binding it up as best he could, he opened the door of his aviary, and his friendly birds flew to greet him with merry roundelay. In the farther corner of the cage he saw something lying stiff and shining. Pax, his milk-white dove, his nearest friend, had died in the night.

CHAPTER III.

NEW ORLEANS is pre-eminent among the cities of the New World for more than one reason. Certain characteristics more European than American are here found, and the mingling of the ceremonious politeness of the French people with the just and liberal spirit of the American has brought about a code of manners superior to that either of France or of our purely American cities. Deference to women still obtains, and the chivalrous attitude of men toward them has not diminished, as in so many parts of our country it has done, in proportion as laws, social and municipal, leave less room for oppression of what is so often called the "weaker sex." Is the phrase a satire, and to-day is the balance of power in the hands of men, or women?

For quaint houses no city in the United States — nay, I had almost said in the world, — can rival New Orleans. The dear queer, rickety little one-story tenements, with rude red terra-cotta tiles and wide eaves leaning over to the edge of the narrow *banquette* (a "side-walk" is an un-

known term in the Crescent City), and the high
dark Spanish buildings, with mysterious pas-
sages leading to hidden courts,— one hesitates
to say which are the most attractive. To Margaret Ruysdale, sculptor, from the North, whose
native New England town was anything but
picturesque, the choice of habitation had been
a difficult one. For days she had wandered
about the streets of the older portion of the city
looking at houses of all degrees.

One morning as she started on her search
she stopped suddenly before a small house which
she had passed perhaps a hundred times, and
had never seen before. It stood on a wide
thoroughfare, which boasted a green ribbon of
turf, running through its middle like a cool, ver-
dant river bordered by two rows of trees. The
large, pretentious dwellings on either side of
the little house seemed to be anxious to elbow
their humbler neighbor out of sight. It stood
back a dozen feet from the street, and with an
effort at self-effacement hid its modest front
behind two straight tall magnolia-trees standing
on either side of the door. When one did at
last obtain a sight of the house, the only wonder
was that one had ever looked at anything else
in all the wide pleasant street. It was a very
low wooden building, of a dull, unaggressive tint
of pearl gray, a story and a half in height. A

piazza ran across the front, with delicately carven pillars and lattice-work. The narrow doorway was flanked by quaint side-lights, through which it was impossible to catch a glimpse of the interior. Overhead, two gable windows leaned gravely over the piazza roof, strewn with leaves fallen from the magnolias. It seemed an ideal dwelling for a maiden, quiet, retired, and yet linked with the busy life of the city, from which it seemed to draw modestly back. Three days later the Ruysdales were settled in the little house, whose interior proved in every way as attractive as Margaret had fancied it to be. Beside the main building there was a large airy room in the rear, which was soon converted into a studio; this was detached, and stood at some distance from the house in a pleasant garden shut in from the thoroughfare in the rear by a high iron fence of very beautiful workmanship. Cunning artificers in iron New Orleans has known, and his must have been a master-hand which moulded the convolvulus vine and flowers twisting about the sheaves of ripe corn in the garden rail. And what a garden it was, with its many tinted roses, one sort for every month in the year, its thick bed of violets all abloom in these first days of February!

Two months have passed since General Stuart Ruysdale and his daughter came to New

Orleans, — the former in search of health, the latter to bear him company. Stuart Ruysdale was not a general in rank; but the loss of his strong right arm in the war had won for him that title with his fellow-townspeople. He had lost more than his right arm in that terrible struggle, — he had lost his health and strength; and he remained for the rest of his days a broken, disappointed man.

When at the breaking out of the Civil War he had been given the commission of captain in a volunteer regiment, Ruysdale had already made some reputation as a sculptor. He had loved his profession with all the passion of a fervent artistic nature springing up in a community where art exists only in its embryonic phase. He had deemed it his mission to nourish that love of the beautiful which is latent in the hearts of men, and to develop sculpture, the greatest of the arts, in his native country, from which he held that all that is best must be evolved, and into which it cannot be imported.

His good right arm had been smitten off, his whole body was maimed and disabled, when, four years later, he came back to Woodbridge at the head of his broken regiment. In his deserted studio he found the tools he could never use again; but in the bitterness of that hour he made a resolve that the power within him should not rest unrevealed, that another hand should give shape to the creations of his brain. The son for whose birth he prayed and looked should be but a finer tool through which his genius should animate the bronze and marble of his native land. He had reckoned, as so many of us do, without his host; for no son was born to him, only a small daughter, who blinked blindly in his face and put out her wee hands to grasp him on the day when her mother died, a month after her birth. Stuart Ruysdale was a man with an iron will. Fate had beaten him at every bout so far, but yield he would not. Son or daughter, his child should be a sculptor; and thus it was that the girl whom Philip Rondelet had met at the house of Mrs. Darius Harden was vowed from her birth a priestess of the plastic art. From her babyhood she had been given wax and clay to model ; and, to the passionate delight of her father, the child showed an unusual aptitude for the profession to which he had dedicated her. Her education had been carried on entirely to this end ; and at twenty, Margaret Ruysdale had certainly produced uncommonly good work for so young a sculptor. Her father's strong conceptions, growing more delicate in passing through the medium of her mind, were to the man like the children of some dear dead child, dearer to him than his own child had been, because of the suffering that had gone before. Margaret loved her profession and her father, the only two things given her to love, with all the strength of her young heart. The two passions were so blended that the serving of the one meant for her the service of the other. There was none of that strife between love and work which vexes so many a woman's life, making the work seem at times a sin, and the love too great a sacrifice.

On a certain soft February afternoon, when the air which stirred the roses outside the studio door was cool and brilliantly pure, Margaret sat at her work while her father, sitting near her, read aloud. The girl had abandoned the bas-relief she had been modelling, and was mould-ing a bird's nest, to the delight of a small negro child seated at her feet.

"How many eggs, General?" whispered Margaret. The child, a son of the cook, had been baptized General Jackson.

"Three, missy," said the baby, holding up the requisite number of fat black fingers.

"'When Angelo heard of the proposed altera-tions in his plans,' — are you paying attention, Margaret?"

"Yes, papa." (*Sotto voce*) "That's the mother bird, General." Inarticulate admiration from General Jackson.

" 'He left Florence in the greatest haste, and repaired to Rome, where he solicited an interview with the Pope — ' "

" Where shall I put the mother bird ? " whispers Margaret.

"On de eggs," answers General Jackson, in the same low voice.

" But that will hide the eggs," objects Margaret.

" Margaret, what are you whispering to that child about ? Can't you send him away ? "

" Yes, papa. Be still, General, can't you ? " very severely.

" 'He found the Holy Father much inclined to coincide with his views, and the difficulties would have been easily smoothed over had it not been for the mischievous intriguing of a certain cardinal — ' "

" See, General, there's the father bird."

" He must have a worm," insisted the child.

" I see there is no use in trying to interest you in Michael Angelo to-day, Margaret. You seem to find that black child vastly more important."

" He is n't quite so remote, papa, and to-day I am rather in a mood for the present ; and General Jackson means the present, don't you, General ? "

" Yes, missy." .

Stuart Ruysdale put the book down, and with

a half-impatient sigh came and stood beside the two culprits. General Jackson looked rather shy, and beat a hasty retreat under Margaret's chair. The young sculptor added the worm to the small bill of the father bird, and placed him in an appropriate attitude by the edge of the nest. Then she laughed.

" Why, you little stupid thing, the birds are not out of the shells yet. What does the father bird bring the worm for ? "

" For de mudder," answered the child promptly, with a shrewd glance at General Ruysdale's sober face.

" Is n't he bright, papa ? "

" I suppose so, my child; but have you been modelling playthings all day, when your Atalanta is in such a condition ? "

Margaret rose, and standing on tiptoe, kissed her father's careworn forehead, mutely asking forgiveness for a neglected duty.

Both the generals soon left her ; and when Philip Rondelet, now a frequent visitor at the house, came into the studio half an hour later, he found Margaret standing at the window with her bird's nest in her hand, looking out into the deepening afternoon sky. He stood watching her a few minutes before he spoke.

" Mademoiselle, what troubles you ? You are sad this afternoon."

"Ah! is it you? I am so glad you have come. I am full of unrest to-day, and it always does me good to see you in these moods," said Margaret, giving him her hand, and forgetting the trace of clay still clinging to it. "Forgive my working woman's hands," she added, with a blush.

"I have always noticed," answered Rondelet, still holding the small firm fingers in his grasp and examining them curiously, "that women who use their hands have a curious false shame at any trace of their work being detected. Coming upon you at your modelling, how could I expect to find your hands like Mrs. Darius Harden's jewelled fingers, white and cared for, lying idly in your lap?"

"Yours are so white, I almost doubt if they ever work."

Rondelet laughed rather uneasily, and changed the conversation.

"You have not answered my question. Why are you troubled and restless to-day?"

"I do not know; I feel a sort of tumult in my blood, — almost a rebellion against existence. And yet I am well and happy, if it is happiness to be without a grief or a care."

"You live too much among your marbles; they chill you."

"But I am feverish, not chilled. I want to be

young.   My youth is slipping from me, and yet
my life is as old and cold as if I carried half
a century of years on my shoulders.   Is it
my fate or my nature which compels me to put
all my life and love into this wet clay, which
absorbs more and more of me each day, and
puts me farther and farther from my kind?   I
want youth and sunlight and foolish gayety.
Take me somewhere where there is something
young!"

She spoke passionately, and threw down her
little modelling tool with a gesture of aversion.
Rondelet, who had learned to know Margaret
Ruysdale very well, had never seen her in such
a humour as this; and for the first time since he
had met her he found it impossible to understand
her, facile as he was in taking the impress of her
thoughts and feelings.   He looked at her, doubtful, embarrassed, not knowing what to say next;
and in that moment of hesitation a shadow fell
between them, — a third person had entered the
studio.   Margaret was looking appealingly into
Philip's face.   He had helped her so often with
his quick sympathy, could he not devise something to soothe this new mood, incomprehensible
to herself as it was to him?   His delicate fair
face flushed painfully beneath her gaze, but he
had nothing to say.

The man who had just come in greeted Ron-

delet and Margaret with a silent bow, and then
stood leaning against the door-post, looking at
the sculptor with inquiring eyes. Margaret
answered the unspoken question with a shake
of her head.

" No, I do not need your services as a model
to-day, Mr. Feuardent ; it is too late to begin to
work. Besides, I am very tired of work ; if you
could take a new *rôle*, now, and help me to play
a little."

" To play ? —why, willingly ; that is the easiest
thing in the world for me. Take off your apron
and come ; we will go to the *fête* at the fair-
grounds and amuse ourselves with the people.
Come, it is a glorious afternoon."

Margaret hastily unfastened and laid aside the
long straight blue apron which hid all the pretty
curves of her small elastic figure.

" Will they be young and happy and alive ? "
she asked.

" We will make them so," answered Feuardent,
with a ringing laugh. " If you and I cannot
stir them up to-day, they must be cold people
indeed."

Margaret answered with a full peal of merriment, and danced away to the house, pausing a
moment to toss General Jackson in her strong
arms.

The two men left together in the studio presented a striking contrast of types. Rondelet, who was well over middle height, looked almost short beside Robert Feuardent, whose great size raised him above the heads of other men. So perfect were his proportions that he always had the effect of dwarfing other people rather than of towering above them. He was a younger man than his companion, and could not have seen more than twenty-five years. His head, which he habitually held rather high, was small and of a Greek mould, and was finely set upon the broad shoulders by a round smooth throat, beautiful as a woman's. His complexion was of the color of a late autumn peach which has hung long upon the tree and acquired a bronze tinge, through which the red shows with a splendid warmth of color. Thick eyebrows, which looked as if they might frown ominously, arched a pair of eyes fearless, open, and with a certain savage beauty, like those of some untamed creature of the woods. His thick dark-brown hair was without curl, but looked full of life and electricity, as did the small mustache which hid the upper lip. When he laughed and showed his small, even, white teeth, the impression of a wild, untamed being was deepened ; it was such a hearty, unconventional laugh, they were such firm, dangerous-looking white teeth. Margaret Ruysdale had told him once that his civilization was only a sham ; that he only masqueraded in broadcloth, and that his proper dress would be a suit of skins.

To the young artist, accustomed to intercourse with people of her own profession and way of thought, this simple natural man, with few broad traits of character and strong instincts and pre-judices, was a constant wonder and amusement. She had understood him instinctively, as Joachim might understand the simple instrument of the Egyptian Fellaheen, two strings stretched over a gourd. But to the peasant musician, the Stradivarius of the master would be a thing of mystery and awe.

So Margaret Ruysdale was to Robert Feuar-dent a perfect enigma. Her delicate, complex nature, fine and strong, impressed him very much. He could not fail to admire her, but neither could he understand her.

Day after day he had sat by and listened while Margaret worked on her bas-relief and conversed with his friend Philip Rondelet of things as foreign to Robert Feuardent as art is foreign to nature.

It was his turn to-day. Rondelet was left outside, wondering and not understanding, and he, Feuardent, had caught the spirit and the meaning of Margaret's mood, as a dark moun-tain lake reflects the image of the maiden moon.

When Robert was sure that Margaret was out of ear-shot, he said in a low voice, —

" I say, Philip, what does Atalanta mean, anyhow ? "

The young physician smiled, and answered, in a tone not quite free from irony, —

" My dear fellow, that's a difficult question. It has puzzled wiser people than you or me. The story goes that many a poor fellow lost his head, in more ways than one, in trying to find out what Atalanta did mean. It's a riddle. Give it up — that's my advice."

" I never was good at riddles," Robert answered gravely, not without a suspicion that his friend was laughing at him. Philip saw this in his face ; and repenting his first impulse to chaff his less erudite friend, was about to enlighten him on the subject of Atalanta's identity, when Robert cried out, " Good-by, Rondelet, I see she is ready ; " and waving his hand to Philip, he ran to meet Margaret, who at that moment appeared on the gallery. Without a word of farewell, Margaret turned, and in a joyous mood sprang down the garden path, with Robert at her side. The iron wicket shut behind them with a sharp snap, and Rondelet was left alone. As he walked toward the house, he heard a shrill cry of grief. General Jackson had broken his bird's nest, and was shrieking inconsolably.

"Bring it here, my boy; I will mend it for you," said Philip. Taking up a morsel of wet clay, he repaired the toy; and warning the child not to play with it till the sun had hardened it, he turned into the house to seek for General Ruysdale.

CHAPTER IV.

RONDELET found General Ruysdale sitting on the shaded porch, watching a passing procession. The elder man greeted him pleasantly, saying,—

"Ah, Rondelet, I was hoping to see you to-day! Do you know we have been in this house just sixty days, and in that time seventy-nine processions have passed before this door?"

"Yes, we are fond of parades here."

"It is such an extravagance. How much better to expend the money devoted to paying those marching musicians in improving the city and carrying on the public charitable institutions, which seem to depend mainly upon private subscription."

"I am not sure about that," Rondelet objected. "It is a great gain to keep the people amused and good-natured. What should we be without our gayety and good-humor? Remember how little we have, poverty-stricken as we are. As to the charities, I hold that the rich and poor are brought in nearer and closer sympathy when they are directly dependent upon

each other. It makes the wealthy realize their
duty to the poor, and the poor look less bitterly
upon a rich class that directly confers benefits
upon them. State charities are such cold, im-
personal things. You rich people at the North
pay taxes to support your sick and blind because
your State forces you to do it, and you avoid
them as much as you can."

The New Englander, high in office over the
charities of his native town, stared at the speaker,
and made an effort to protest against these he-
retical remarks. But Rondelet continued, —

" You think us behind the world in every
way, behind the North particularly. Well, perhaps we are ; but the social atmosphere which
your condition of things has brought about is
not without its drawbacks. The aristocracy of
money, which rules your society with a golden
rod, is not, to my mind, a noble or great phase
of human existence. ·You are now suffering
from a very plethora of money, a terrible indi-
gestion from too much high living, while we are
growing day by day weaker and weaker from
inanition ; and yet you would have us call you
brothers ! Our country is one now, and I hope
and believe will ever remain so ; but the country cannot march as it should in the progress of
nations while one foot is bare, lame, and blis-
tered. It is strange that you forget us so ; our

interests are bound up with yours, there is no
separating them. That has been proved, and
the proof was a grave one, as you who shed
your blood, as I who lost my patrimony in the
awful proving, know full well."

"But you brought it on yourselves, after all.
As you made your bed, so must you lie on it.
Can a parent love the child that has turned and
struck at her life, as she does the one that gave
his own to defend it?"

"Do you remember the parable of the prodigal
son? Methinks that the husks have been fed
to us too long, and that, despite the well-fed
elder brother, the fatted calf should be slain.
But, General, I did not come to talk politics with
you, sir, but to take my revenge for my defeat of
last evening. Are you in the mood for a game
of chess?"

It was as well that Rondelet had turned the
conversation, as it might soon have become a
heated one. The bitterness which had crept
into his voice was most unusual with him. In
all his intercourse with the old officer, he had
never shown the feeling he had just expressed.
It is not improbable that this state of mind was
produced by what had gone before in the studio.
The General was too well-bred a man not to
abandon the topic, though it cost him something
of a struggle to do so. He was one of those

natural fighters, to whom a contest of words is next best to that of arms.

"I will play a game of chess with pleasure," he answered. "There is one thing I wish to speak to you about first, Rondelet; it is about the killing of young Fernand Thoron. Have you heard of any new developments in the case?"

The General watched the young physician keenly as he spoke. Philip's color changed as he answered, in a low, constrained voice, —

"No, I have heard nothing."

"They were talking about it at the club last night; no one told you of that?"

"No."

"I think you ought to know," said the General, speaking slowly and impressively, "what was said — whispered, rather, for I do not know how the rumor started, or even how it reached my ears; but it was suggested by some one that you knew something about that affair."

It had come at last, the vague report of that wild night, nearly two months ago. He straightened himself where he stood, as if to brace himself against another shock. But the General said nothing more, and evidently waited for an answer. It came slowly.

"I never to my knowledge saw the man you speak of. I remember hearing of his sudden death at the time, and that a theory of suicide was very generally accepted. Did you know him? What did he look like?"

" I had seen him once only. He was a fine-looking fellow and quite young. Margaret had met him, and he brought his mastiff, Launce, a fine dog, for her to model in her Atalanta. She was much shocked to hear of his death three days after."

" His mastiff Launce, a fine dog," these words sounded dimly in Rondelet's ears. They settled the question which had so long tormented him as to the identity of Fernand Thoron and the youth he had seen die in the hut near the duelling ground. He had avoided seeking the solution of the mystery, remembering Jean's words, " It is better for you that you should not know;" but now the knowledge was forced upon him, and with it a sense of the suspicion with which he was regarded. The General's eyes were still fixed upon Rondelet inquiringly, but he had nothing more to say.

" Shall we have our game?"

" Certainly," said the General, placing the men upon the board ; and the battle began.

At the moment when the two gentlemen were arranging their chessmen, Margaret and Robert entered the Fair Grounds. The scene that met their eyes was an animated one. A vast crowd of gayly dressed people filled the large enclosure, where numbers of booths and ornamented tents flaunted their banners and streamers in the evening air. Here a band of fortune-tellers professed to predict the future of young men and maidens for a small compensation. These gypsy folk had established themselves at the foot of a giant live-oak, whose wide-spreading arms served to shelter them from the rays of the afternoon sun.

A girl tricked out with tinsel and mock jewels beckoned to Margaret and Robert, and with a bold smile dropped them a courtesy and invited them to approach and have their fortune told; but the two passed on unheeding. A wonderful glittering palace, with a retinue of beasts, next attracted their attention, — a pair of elephants, followed by twin ostriches, with dolphins, giraffes, deer, winged horses, goats, unicorns, half the animals of history and fable, slowly gyrating to the strains of some concealed music.

"Will you ride in the great show? Only a nickel apiece!" cried the showman in a voice made harsh by long vociferation. The pair stood back and watched the riders who bestrode the strange creatures. When the number of travellers was complete, the music pealed forth in quicker time, and the whole Noah's ark seemed to take unto itself wings, and flew round and round at a bewildering pace. Beyond the

revolving palace a crowd of people stood watching the brightening sky.   A small black box
suddenly appeared, whirling upwards at a great
speed ; then came an explosion ; and a gigantic
uncouth monster, idol or demon, floated slowly
earthward, assuming successive clumsy attitudes
in its descent, now bowing gravely, again doub-
ling itself up, as in a very paroxysm of infernal
laughter at the crowd beneath, who screamed
and applauded with shout and halloo.

"It is too ugly," cried Robert; "its horrid
shadow must not fall on you.   Away ! away !"

" Look again !" said Margaret ; " see the pal-
ette of the cloud-painter."

This time the square black box had thrown
out a little group of colors, to the number of
seven.   These grew and grew, till they seemed
like so many tinted clouds floating westward
toward the sunset, which now began to flame
forth from the crystal sky.

"To the dancers !" cried Robert. "Come while
there is yet time ; it will soon be night." And
taking the hand of his companion, he hurried her
toward a spot where a group of people were
weaving the intricate patterns of a contra-dance.
Thrusting aside the crowd of on-lookers, he
quickly found a place for himself and his partner,
and they struck into the measure with a frank
delight which animated the dancers as a mag-

netic shock electrifies a whole circle of linked human beings. They hardly recognized each other, this quiet, hard-working maiden, and this melancholy, brooding man, who had for weeks met and parted every day, each speaking his own language and ignorant of the other's as of a foreign tongue. At last they understood each other, and the contagious gayety of the pair set the whole line of dancing folk into a sympathetic merriment. The master of ceremonies was in despair as the couples, abandoning the set figures, which he called aloud in a persuasive voice, followed the new-comers through quaint and intricate measures never trod before. It seemed as if Terpsichore had abandoned her sex and was masquerading in the form of this tall fellow, who looked the very incarnation of the dance as he led the merry throng through march and counter march, flourish, promenade, galop, and at last the waltz, which Robert started, catching his lithe, tireless partner in his arms and whirling her to its wavy measures. His dark face was flushed with the passion of the dance, and faster and faster he whirled his light burden through the swaying maze of men and maids. "Enough, enough!" cried a youth, and the cry was repeated; it seemed as if they could not leave the mad whirl into which he had led them without the signal from this self-appointed master of the revels. He heeded not the exclamations of the crowd ; but suddenly conscious of the tremulous throbbing of the heart beating so near to his, he halted in the midst of the dreamy exaltation.

"You will die if we do not stop," he said, looking at Margaret's dilated eyes and panting breast.

"Such a dance is worth a life," she answered ; and laughed, and panted for her lost breath. He drew her from the crowd and placed her on a seat beneath an arbor shaded by a group of heavy-scented magnolia-trees. She drew her breath with labored gasps, growing less and less frequent, and he fanned her with a branch of green leaves.

"Have I found you what you needed ? "

"Yes, yes ; it was what I dreamed of."

"I have made you feel young and happy and alive ? "

" Yes."

"When you need youth and happiness and life again, will you send for me ? "

She nodded.

"Always ? "

"*Always ?* Don't talk about anything so serious ! *Always* means to-morrow, next week, next year, the future, and that most terrible thought the mind can conceive, — Eternity ! Let me have to-day to myself undisturbed, will you not ? "

" Ay."

Sitting in the arbor, looking westward, they watched the fading sky grow faint and color-less, and then deepen with the beauty of the night, purple, gold-flecked. From the dark mag-nolia overhead the mocking-bird trilled forth his matchless thread of song, linking the gems of heaven with the star flowers of earth. The per-fume of the flowers was full of a subtile intoxica-tion ; and under the fitful light of the many-colored lanterns hanging from the branches like vast lu-minous fruits, pairs of men and women appeared and disappeared, flitting down the dim rose-bordered alleys. Strangers yesterday, strangers again perhaps to-morrow, but for that hour lov-ers, — by the power of the night, the odor of the flowers, by the note of the mocking-bird, and beneath all these by the magic melody of the Spring throbbing in the breasts of men, kindling in the eyes of girls, gushing from the song-bird's throat, swimming from the hearts of flowers, Spring and Love, Love and Spring!

The music of a hidden orchestra took up the great hymn, and the viols wailed forth the pas-sion of that noblest of love-songs, " Adelaida," whose measures the deaf Beethoven never heard.

The throng grew greater ; dark-eyed girls in soft-hued garments of state trod the sanded paths with satin-shod feet: the wedding-guests had come from a church near by. Now that the bride no longer needed their gentle ministrations, the eight fair bridesmaidens joined the *fête*. They walked sedately two by two, fresh as the flowers of the field which they typified. This yellow dandelion, nodding gayly as she passes, has the dark eyes and rounded limbs of the South ; but her cheeks are red with the color of the northern rose. She laughs ; and catching sight of Robert, greets him with a, —

· " Bon soir, Robert le diable."

" She is a working-woman, as *you* call yourself," he whispers ; "she does the work and earns the salary of a man."

A blue field-flower passes, graceful, slight, with lips that curl a little scornfully sometimes ; but to-night they smile as she hums the melody of the song.

" That young girl is a musician, and earns her bread too, though she is so young."

A scarlet poppy follows. She has a fine, sensitive face, red-bronze hair, and determined brown eyes.

" Her father lost his fortune and his life at the close of the war. She it is who has educated her sisters and kept her brothers to their duty. Her

fingers are never idle ; besides clothing her many
sisters, she finds time to fashion garments for
some gentlewomen poorer than she, and not
less proud."

"That morning-glory is well fitted to typify
the flower she wears," said Margaret.

"Yes ; she is to be the maiden queen of our
carnival revels."

"She is very beautiful, but she looks almost
too slight to bear the burden even of a crown
of pleasure."

"You will see her carry her honors regally, and
yet modestly."

The living chain of flowers linked together
two by two passed gayly by, and were soon lost
in the surging crowd of holiday folk. The *fête*
was at its height, and our two pilgrims of pleasure felt this hour to be the fairest of the day as
they sat a little withdrawn from the current of
passing people, and yet not out of sympathy with
them. Robert, leaning back, with the soft leaves
of the jessamine-vine touching his cheek, gave a
sigh of pleasure, and after a short pause spoke
again to his companion, just for the happiness of
hearing her voice in answer to his question.

"Life is pleasant to you now ? "

"Yes, very, very pleasant ; and I believe that I
have earned the right to enjoy it. It is very long
since I have played."

"Yes, it is a glorious thing, life, on such a night as this. There are many pleasures which we often forget to be grateful for."

Something touched him on the shoulder. It was a touch as light as the tap of the leaves against him; but he started as if some one had struck him a direful blow. A voice faint as the wind echoing in the trees whispered these words in his ear: "Those who die in strife leave behind the pleasures, but not the pain of life."

The young man started to his feet and crossed himself mechanically. Through the thicket he caught a glimpse of a tall woman with a mantilla wrapped about her head and shoulders; at the sight the color faded from his lip and cheek, and his great frame shook with a sudden tremor. Margaret had seen and heard nothing; but she rose and shivered even as he had done, and laying her hand upon his arm said, "Take me home; we have stayed too long."

CHAPTER V.

MARGARET had received her first commission! What artist does not remember the day when he sold his first picture? What sculptor but has made a broad red mark in his memory against the day his first model was accepted? What writer can recall without a smile of reflected pleasure the hour when the post brought him, not his own carefully written manuscript, "returned with regrets and thanks," but a letter telling him that his thoughts are to be scattered abroad to the world through the mighty medium of the printing-press? He may learn later that what he thought was living seed is nothing but chaff, thrown out from other brains, and mistaken by him for original inspiration; he may find that the seed, though living, falls upon stony ground, and perishes. But in that hour of maiden success there is no gnawing doubt of self; all is pure, triumphant happiness. Perhaps only second to one moment in all our lives is this first victory, — that moment when the one heart in all the world whose beating is attuned to our own acknowledges the sweet concord, and we know that the two can never again be entirely divided.

Margaret had received her first commission. Her voice was heard singing a happy little tune over the work which, from that time forth, acquired a new dignity in her eyes. It had a market value. It was merchantable, like sugar and cotton, bricks and breadstuffs. Men would exchange that which they love best after — and sometimes before — their own souls for its possession. She was an amateur no longer. She had become a money-getter, a bread-winner, a producer. The mere fact that she was to get so many dollars for fulfilling the order would not have accounted for the exhilaration of Margaret's spirits. It would be hard to imagine a person to whom the possession of wealth was of less importance. She had never wanted for anything in her life. Her tastes were simple. She gave away half the income which was settled on herself because she did not care to take the time or thought to spend it. She was not an heiress, but had a sufficient fortune to maintain her comfortably all her days. Money meant only to her what it does to those who have neither suffered the need of it nor felt the embarrassment of its excess. There must have been some reason, then, for Margaret's happiness, beyond the mere prospect of winning a certain number of bank-notes. What is this feeling which urges the queen on her throne to put her thoughts into merchantable shape and offer them to be sold at a stall alongside the book of some humble writer starving in a garret? What induces a princess of the blood to hang her pictures in the great exhibitions, laying aside her royalty for the nonce, and claiming equality with her artist subjects? It is a strange instinct, this; it seems like an acknowledgment that in proportion as a thing is salable, so is it valuable. And yet Theodore Winthrop died broken-hearted, his three noble books, still in manuscript, rejected by every publisher in the land, while authors of certain dime-novels of his time have grown rich through the sale of their very unsavory works.

Why Margaret was so happy, the recorder of her triumph cannot say, and must leave the question to the reader, trusting that he may find the proper solution of this problem.

It was a curious order, the like of which it is doubtful if ever sculptor was intrusted with.

Perhaps the nearest parallel to it that the history of art affords is the snow statue commanded from Michael Angelo by the Medici. Tradition says that though Angelo received the order of his patron with a very bad grace, he nevertheless executed it with his never-failing skill. I have never known, but have always wondered what subject the sculptor chose to typify in the fleeting marble of the snowdrift. May he not have moulded an image of the god Eros, youngest, fairest, most remorseless of the Olympians, whose touch, like that of the snow, at once burns and freezes?

Margaret was commissioned to summon forth from the depths of a salt-mine its tutelary deity; and having once seen its face, to sculpture it on the living wall of its invaded domain. She visited the mine; and what she saw and learned there can be best told in her own words. We take the liberty of making an extract from Miss Ruysdale's private journal : —

PAGES FROM THE DIARY OF MARGARET RUYSDALE.

" The order is now given to make ready the lift, and in a twinkling we find ourselves dropping out of the light of day, below the surface of the earth. Swiftly but steadily the small square platform drops down, down, into the bosom of the earth. The motion is so rapid that we seem to be flying from the daylight. At the bottom of the shaft we alight, to find ourselves in the upper gallery of the salt-mine. It is Sunday, and the great shining corridor, hewn out of the pure crystal, is silent and without sign of life. A group of flickering oil-lamps stand prepared for us, and each of us hastens to take possession of one, eager to keep back the great sea of darkness by the small beacon of a miner's lamp.

"The vaulted roof is upborne by gigantesque pillars sculptured from the living crystal, and we pass down the wide aisles full of a wonder not untouched by awe. Leading the way is one slight figure, which we might well imagine to be that of the genius of the mine, — a young woman, whose graceful form assumes at each instant some new and classic pose. She now holds her lamp high above her head, to show a splendid crystal shining like a diamond on the side of the mine, and again stoops to pick a fragment of rock-salt from the floor. As she pauses and looks over her shoulder at us who follow, she recalls one of the figures which Pompeii has preserved on the walls of its ruined villas, graceful, airy, with the careless, light beauty of Greek art domiciled in Italy. As we turn into one of the branching galleries, a new spectacle meets our view. High up against the roof a faint light glimmers out of the heavy darkness. It grows stronger and brighter, and at last springs into a triumphant glory, illuminating vaulted roof and pillared aisle, floor, and shining walls with its warm glow. It sparkles on the wondrous crystals, and reveals the great drilled holes of the blasts ; it throws itself triumphantly down the midnight gallery, and is lost in its distant shadows ; it touches the face of a youth, beautiful as a young faun, who bends close beside the flame and feeds it with a steady hand.' It is dynamite, this rosy, searching radiance, and the young man is its guardian. The light wanes slowly, and at last flickers out, and the shadows come trooping about us again thick and fast.

" The others are going to another part of the mine ; but I linger behind them, unwilling to leave so soon this strange place. They have turned into the main aisle again ; the voices and torches grow fainter and dimmer, and are finally lost. Moved by a sudden impulse, I quench the small spark of light I carry in my hand, and the darkness settles visibly about me like a pall. It presses upon my shoulders with an irresistible weight, and forces me to my knees upon the soft, salt-sanded earth. I cannot stand alone in this wonderful quiet darkness. A power that I have never felt before compels me to bend my head before the Invisible. My life, it seems to me, was in some mysterious way burning with that tiny point of flame in the vase of oil. With the failing of the flame my life has been extinguished, and I am now nothing but a shadow, like those that fled before me but a moment ago. Will the flame ever be rekindled? Shall I ever again reclaim my lost humanity? And if I could, would I raise my voice to make that claim heard? There is a pause unmeasured by sight or sound. Is it of minutes or of centuries? Am I still a human being, or a shadow of the mine? No senses are left me, but a power of vision which is not of the senses.

" I am conscious of a vast plain of water, blue, tranquil, limitless, waveless, for it is a sea without a shore ; and in the heaven shines a spotless sun, calm, radiant, all-powerful. Time passes ; are they seconds or eons

that elapse before the sapphire sea is troubled and
broken into crested lines of white sea-foam? Dark
streaks seem trembling upwards, striving with and at
last conquering the all-powerful sea; for a low ridge of
land appears, defying the waters, which must now for
all time fret and chafe against its stubborn sides. The
brown streaks grow and grow, stretch out towards
each other, and link themselves at last into a great
ring, prisoning in its midst a disk of 'conquered
water. In vain the bounded sea rebels and tries to
break down the wall of earth that holds it fast, and
rush back to its mother element. In vain; for it is
the day when God said, 'Let there be land!' And
the ring grows broad, and strong, and firm, and at last
beautiful and green; for the great sun is its friend, and
the lake is land-locked, — a hopeless captive. But
while the sun looks kindly on the earth, and brings
forth from its bosom strange and beautiful forms, it
parches the lake cruelly, and the prisoner pines and
shrinks, and grows less and less, while the eager land
presses greedily about it, and follows its retreat step
by step; and at every step which the land gains there
is a mark of its victory, a mark that shall endure while
the land exists. But the bitterness of the sea cannot
be conquered; and when the victory is complete, and
the last lapse of water has dried and died beneath the
sun, the land bears in its bosom a great basin of sea-
salt, which testifies to those who shall come thereafter
that the sea once held dominion here. But all is not
peaceful yet with the conquering land. Stormy passions shake her being, and in one of these outbursts of

volcanic fury the great salt basin is torn from its bed
and tossed upon its side, and so lies edgewise ; for the
earth cannot expel, though she may distort, the legacy
of the sea.   And now the land covers that which she
cannot cast out with clean, soft soil, and a wondrous
thick carpet of green, from which spring giant trees
and fair flowers, making the land full of beauty to him
who has come at last to enjoy all that has been so long
preparing for him.   Man comes, and with him human
labor ; and the soil is tilled, and cane is planted, and
bears sugar for the master of the land.   But the hidden salt is still there, and the roots of the cane reach
far down into the earth.   And when the cane is gathered, and the stubble stands through the long winter, a
strange, white bloom is seen upon its broken stumps,
which when tasted proves to be, not sweet, but salt.
The black laborer learns this fact without question.
By the simpler types of man all the wonders of nature
are thus accepted, one seeming not more mysterious
than another.   And the land still keeps her secret.

"A well is needed, and a shaft is sunk.   Water
comes bubbling to the surface, bringing with it a
strange testimony of the forgotten sea ; the spring is
salt.   Time passes ; the golden age of peaceful agri-
culture comes and goes, and Acadia knows the iron
age of war.   War and want frown down upon the
strong young country.   The great storehouses of the
world are closed, and men are thrown back upon
the resources of their own land.   There is a salt famine ; and a man who thinks more than his neighbors
brings the great kettles from his sugar-house and boils

the water of the salt spring, and thus secures a small supply of salt. This is while the latest of the centuries is in its youth and the youngest of the nations in its childhood. Peace again! And commerce comes back, bringing its supplies from other countries, and saving men the toil of seeking at home that which it is easier to bring from abroad. The salt spring is forgotten, and half a century passes before the red war-cloud darkens above Arcadia. War again, the cruellest of all wars, in which the lusty sons have turned their weapons each against his brother; there is no other strong enough to cope with them. Then the dwellers in the island remember the tradition of the boiling of the salt water, and the old kettles are set up again, and a meagre residuum of salt is gained, while the great basin lies unsuspected ten feet beneath the surface of the ground. The spring fails one day, and a new well is sunk. The laborers strike, in digging it, a rock which they cannot dislodge.

" ' Dig around it,' says the overseer. Dig around it! Dig around the great salt basin whose upper edge it takes a hundred and a half acres of soil to cover! The task is soon seen to be a difficult one, and the obstinate ledge of rock, which cannot be dug around, is examined. At last, after cycles have passed, you are avenged, O sea! and the land is found to be but a setting to the great treasure she holds embedded in her jealous breast. Pure and priceless in its worth is the great salt-bed, and the island which was never heard of before a hundred miles beyond its shores is now one of the wonders of the New World,

"A light breaks upon my eyes, which have forgotten the darkness in the great panorama which has been spread before my mind. I struggle to my feet, and in a moment am surrounded by my friends, who have not had time even to notice my absence. It was but for a half-hour, after all, that I was lost in the salt-mine."

After this preliminary visit followed days of earnest work, during which the studio door yielded not to the touch of friend or admirer, Margaret's father even being for the first time excluded from her counsels. Hitherto she had labored mainly to please him, and had worked under his direction, carrying out his ideas. She had been, in very fact, little more than the fine tool he had fashioned for himself. All was now changed. Her individuality must play its part ; she would be held responsible for her work, and her brain alone must direct her hand. For the first time in her life she felt the creative force in herself. The clay seemed a living substance, which moulded itself beneath her hands as if as much interested as she in the process of its transformation. When her model was complete, Margaret and her father disappeared from the city, accompanied by a kindred spirit, whom Margaret had discovered in the person of one Antonio, a master stonecutter famous for his tasteful mantelpieces and mortuary monuments.

No warning was given of their intended departure, and their friends were at a loss to account
for it. Gradually the secret leaked out, and a
conspiracy was formed to follow the fugitives
to the very bowels of the earth.

Mrs. Harden was the prime leader of the
enterprise, and the party included Philip Rondelet. Feuardent was not invited. Meanwhile
Margaret, quite unconscious of the plot for her
pursuit, was working steadily. The days flew
by as only working days do, when each hour
sees something accomplished, each day a step
hewn out of the mountain road at whose summit Fame sits. To some men it is an easy
ascent ; they reach the top without suspecting it.
It is told of Rossini (whose early operas had
been hissed from the stage) that on the night
when that masterpiece, "The Barber of Seville,"
was first produced, he dared not go to the the-
atre, but sat at home shivering in his poor room.
Presently he heard the sound of a great throng
of people in the street below — on the stair — at
his very door. "They have come to mob me !"
cried the great composer ; and as no other escape was possible, he beat a hasty retreat up the
chimney. They came and bade him stand forth
to receive the homage of the whole city assembled
to do him honor.

I knew a man once, a famous writer to-day,

whose fears of public ridicule it was my task
to strive to allay while his first book was in
press. Three months after, his name was known
wherever the English language is read. There
are men who walk steadily down the scale of
excellence, as unconscious of their descent as
this other was of his upward progress. There
are those again, in the band of mountaineers
striving to reach the Alpine summit, who through
their own temerity lose foot-hold and slip head-
long into some abyss. To such a one it often
happens that his more fortunate companions
lower ropes to him and strive in every way to
extricate him from the pit into which he has
fallen. If they succeed in bringing him to the
surface, they try to shoulder him along with
themselves. That is a pleasant phase, and one
that I like to see ; never mind if the rescued man
should slip into the next crevasse, his friends
will be all the better able to go on their way for
having given him another chance. The cautious
man, who sits down on the safe ground of his
first successful step and dares go no farther lest
the crust should give way beneath his feet, is,
alas ! a common type, and perhaps the saddest
one to see. We expected so much of him ! His
first book struck so fine a note, ringing out clear
and bold, penetrating the busy ears dulled by
constant world-rumble. We cry, "Bravo! Go on!

Give us the second note in the chord!" But the second note is the first! Like Toto's kingly singer, he can go no farther than Do! He can roar it louder and louder, *do!* DO! DO! but he cannot sing *re!* though he should split his throat.

We can make no symphony of praise for him; he gave the key-note, others must make the harmony. It is painful of ascent at best, this hill, even where ambition is the staff, and the heels are winged with genius. It is too rough a road for a woman to tread, and let us hope that our young heroine will not attempt it. Better for her the smooth country by-road, with fruitful fields on either hand, than the rugged mountain path. And yet " Mr. Toil" is the only spouse who is never unfaithful; and when friend, sweetheart, husband, break troth with a woman, let her open her arms and fold the grim old fellow to her deserted breast. If she be true to him, he will not forsake her in the darkest hour. The more homage she laid at the feet of the mortal lover, the colder he grew, perchance; but with " Mr. Toil " every sacrifice is richly rewarded, the closer the embrace in which she folds him, the stronger the support he returns.

None of these thoughts troubled Margaret Ruysdale, one may be sure, as she sat high up on her scaffolding in the dark gallery of the salt-mine. They are thoughts which do not vex children, and the young girl was, as her friend Sara Harden often said, still a child in most respects. The work was finished. That very night the scaffolding was to be knocked away. Her fingers lingered lovingly over the surface which she should never touch again. With her chisel she deepened a line here, and shaved off a particle of crystal there. She was taking farewell of the face which she had freed from the living wall of salt. How she had enjoyed cutting the clear white crystal from the features which she almost believed were behind it!

"I am only unveiling the face of the salt-spirit," she had said a dozen times when her father and the cutter of stone had warned her that she was working too hastily in the brittle material. She had understood instinctively the soft, friable, salt crystal, and had used her chisel with more dexterity than her colleague, hampered by the traditions of his trade.

"None but a novice would have attempted it," said the workman admiringly. "A novice and a woman! Only novices and women achieve the impossible."

"And genius, Antonio," added the General sententiously, claiming for his daughter the supreme of gifts. Stuart Ruysdale was a modest man as far as he himself was concerned; but his vanity in regard to his child was unbounded. The most unassuming people often make the vainest parents.

A group of moving lights appeared at the end of the gallery. Margaret supposed they were carried by a party of miners, and paid no heed to their approach. The lights halted at the foot of the scaffolding, and still she went on retouching the features with a loving care. There was a pause, then a shout of greeting fell upon her ear. She started; and being perilously near the edge of the planking, gave a little cry of fright before she could answer the salutation. When she learned that her friends had come to visit her, she made her way down the ladder. Philip was the first to take her hand.

" How could you deceive me so ? " he asked.

" I did n't; I only let you be deceived."

" Beshrew you for an evil-disposed little thing. I wonder you dared come down at all. Do you call this the part of friendship?" cried Mrs. Harden.

" Forgive me, all of you ! I did want to keep my secret to myself, and you have got the better of me, after all ; so be magnanimous."

" It will depend upon how we like your Lot's wife. It's that, of course, you have been digging out of the wall ? " rejoined Mrs. Harden, laughing.

"You shall see," answered Margaret. "They have come to take away the supports, and you shall guess what the subject is."

When the obscuring planks were removed, a strong light was cast upon the roof of the mine, which was vaulted, like the aisle of a Norman church. Vast pillars hewn out of the quartz, spanned by round arches, supported the roof; and near one of these massive columns Margaret had carved the likeness of the salt-sprite. The face on which the brilliant flickering light now fell was set about with glittering salt-crystals, which shone like so many mammoth diamonds. It was a melancholy face, full of startled surprise. From the darkness of the mine it glimmered forth, pale, reproachful, ghostly.

"How beautiful, but how uncanny! Where did you ever see such a face, child?" said Mrs. Harden, breaking the silence.

"Here in the mine."

"It is a great success," said the master of the mine, "and I congratulate myself on the possession of so remarkable a work of art. My only regret is that it exists in so perishable a material."

Each one had his or her word to say of praise and gratulation. General Ruysdale, pleased and proud, walked about, viewing the sculptured head from every point, "positively chortling with happiness," as Mrs. Harden said ; but Margaret soon slipped away from her friends and admirers. Philip followed, and found her sitting near the shaft, in the twilight region, where the darkness of the mine and the glad light of day were struggling for the upper hand.

"Are you not satisfied?" he asked, quick to see her trouble.

"No, and it hurts me to have you all praise it when I know how much better I could have made it. It seems as if you expected nothing more of me, and were surprised that I have done even as well as this."

"Dear friend, believe me, that feeling is one that you will always have, no matter at what point you may arrive in your art. You have in your own mind the spirit of the conception, and, do what you will, you can only show us its reflection. When self-satisfaction comes, progress stops. May you never know it."

"It makes me ashamed to have them praise me," Margaret repeated. And Philip laughed, and told her that this was as it should be.

CHAPTER VI.

THE Carnival was at hand, and the city was tingling with curiosity and expectation of the pranks the revellers were preparing to perpetrate. Practical jokes of the most complex nature were brewing in the minds of men whose age and occupation might in other parts of the world have precluded the possibility of their taking part in such frivolous amusement. Canal Street was crowded with shoppers, *flaneurs*, and loafers of all degrees, from the gentlemen congregated about the steps of the Club-house to the knot of unaccountables at the street corner. Nowhere in the world does the verb "to loaf" exist in so many tenses as in New Orleans; not dreamy Venice, nor sunny Naples itself, can excel the Crescent City in the number of its loafers or the quality of its loafing. It is an art, indeed, to loaf well and elegantly, so that the action is without irritating effect upon work-driven unfortunates, or repellantly suggestive of the waste of time to those who by nature resemble that tiresome, overrated insect, the busy bee.

Ask this same hard-working honey-bee if he would n't like to be a drone if he could. I warrant he would jump, or fly, or buzz, or do whatever a bee does to express pleasure at the chance to change places with the favored attendant of the queen-bee.

One evening, when Canal Street was even more crowded with loafers than is its wont, two persons, who seemed to have some definite object in being abroad, took their way down this wide thoroughfare, the main artery through which the city's life-blood pulsates. Philip Rondelet and his companion, Margaret Ruysdale, would gladly have joined the throng of wayfarers loitering through the street; but as neither ventured to make the suggestion, they followed the programme they had marked out for the evening. Leaving the gay highway, they turned into a narrow alley which led through one of the poorest quarters of the town. There were no street-lamps here, only an occasional lantern swinging before the door of some dealer in liquors or small wares. At the corner of a cross street they paused for a moment, attracted by the interior of a small shop where a bright light was flaring. Heaps of vegetables and fruit were piled against the walls, and from the darkened rafters hung bunches of herbs and red peppers. A fire burned on the hearth, over which a pot was suspended by a rusty iron chain. A woman with a red handkerchief drawn over her head was superintending the cooking. She was no longer young, but showed traces of beauty in the outlines of her face and figure. She was of a Spanish type ; but that her blood was not unmixed with that of an inferior race was evident from the too deep olive of the skin and the closely curling hair. A man sat near her on the counter engaged in sharpening a knife on a small grindstone. It was a harmless knife, fit only for the paring of vegetables ; but in the hands of the red-shirted *dago* it seemed to lose its innocent character, his fierce dark face was so intent upon his work, his strong bare arm looked as if it could wield a more dangerous blade so effectively. The two were listening to a third person, who completed the group, a woman who might have been sister or daughter to her of the red handkerchief, judging from her profile. In a moment she turned to the man, who was delicately testing the blade of his knife upon his fingers ; and as she moved toward him, the full light, falling upon her, revealed a white, eager face, framed in heavy black hair and marked by straight dark eyebrows. The resemblance had vanished ; there could be no kinship surely between this tall young woman, with her white jewelled hands and simple mourning robe of

modish design and the quadroon woman with
her rough companion; and yet the eyes of all
three had a curious resemblance, rising slightly
at the corners, their color a deep fiery brown
that was not without a tinge of red. The
younger woman was evidently appealing to the
man, for he shook his head and made a sign
of dissent, shaking the forefinger of his right
hand, and then setting to work on his knife
again. The elder woman said something, in a
language unknown to Margaret, in a soothing
tone. The younger one answered passionately
and with a despairing gesture.

"Theresita, be quiet; let's hear no more
about killing," said the man in a hoarse undertone. "Have n't you seen enough of that sort
of business yet?"

The two in the street had paused outside, attracted by the picturesque interior, with its three
striking figures. At these significant words
Margaret started and turned to go. Rondelet
stood perfectly still, his eyes fixed upon Therese,
in whom he recognized the heroine of that
strange adventure at the old duelling-ground.

Margaret touched him. "Come away," she
whispered, appealingly.

Philip started, drew her arm through his own,
and hurried her from the place, looking back
over his shoulder as he walked.

" What did it all mean ? " she asked presently.

" God knows, my child. Promise me to forget it, — never to think of it or speak of it again."

" I can never forget that woman's face ; I will not speak of it."

" I had no right to bring you through such a neighborhood. Ah, here is your church at last."

They entered a large square meeting-house, before which were flaring several pine-wood torches. Half a dozen blacks were loafing about the entrance ; but the love-feast was too attractive to permit of many of the congregation's loitering outside the church. Margaret and Rondelet took their seats just as the preacher rose to his feet. He was a mulatto, with a clever face and a certain magnetism which made itself felt as soon as he opened his lips. The words of his text were, " The man that is perfect in his dealings, it is not a hard matter for him to get a living in this world. Therefore be perfect in all your dealings ; and to be perfect you must be of one mind."

" The Apostle Paul says, ' Be of one mind.' Week after week you have a little preacher that stands here talking to you ; what is he for ? To get all your hearts centred on one thing, — the grace of God, that you may live again in peace, that you may be of one mind. That is the question, that is the question, — of one mind.

Would it not be a good plan to be of one mind to take hold of a rope? You have seen men pulling on a cable. All get on the rope. If all pull one way, they move a great weight. But suppose one turns his face another way: they won't move much. Now in a class-meeting, if we are of one mind, and that mind the salvation of men's souls, can we not do a great work? Jesus says you can move a mountain. You can ask God for any service; you can ask God to convert any young man. He will do it.

" What a great comfort it is when a young man or woman who desires his salvation may come and see there are so many prayers going up in their behalf. God will answer prayer. God will take the sinner out of his own ways ; ' he will place a new song in his mouth.'

" Any person that don't pray, can't be comfortable. By praying, a man or woman in the dark hours of midnight feels comforted when he wrestles with God. Some of you have witnessed this. Waking up in the night,—you get up in the dark, you wrestle with God in a sorrow and prayer, and he answers your prayer. You feel comfort in the Holy Spirit. But a person that don't pray can't feel comfortable. Ask a sinner man or sinner woman, ask him if a pain strikes him; he is not comfortable. But the child of God can bear the pain with comfort. The first thing his mind calls on is his Jesus. The first thing that strikes the sinner is God's judgment, —'I have offended God, I am troubled !' And for that poor sinner, if I can sing in his ears, there is good comfort. Live in peace ; the God of love and peace shall be with you. Don't you want this peace? Don't you want a perfect body,—perfect before man, perfect before God ? If there is anything the Old Man hates, it is to see a young man stand up and say he is going to be free. There is a little fear of Catholics in the second order going wrong, because they give a penalty on you ; but in God's Church you are so free you let the penalty fall on your souls. Be perfect in your dealings, be true to one another ; then it will be the consequence : the God of love and peace shall be with you, if you be perfect in these meetings. I have no fault to find; I can find fault after fault if I want. The best man that ever lived has done some fault ; but the man that is perfect, — the man that is perfect in his dealings, — it is not a hard matter for him to get a living in the world. Be perfect in all your dealings ; and to be perfect you must be of one mind. And in the next world, oh, my beloved sisters and brothers, we will part no more ! There will be comfort and happiness, and the day of wrestling with God will be past, when we get to heaven, when we get to heaven !"

The minister had begun his discourse quietly and fervently ; but as he spoke he became more animated. His voice was of a sonorous quality and of unusual capacity. As he drew near to the close of his address he was frequently interrupted by cries of " Glory, glory ! That 's so ! Oh, my soul ! Poor sinners ! " These ejaculations acted as stimulants to the preacher, and his voice now grew soft and thrilling, and again pealed forth like a trumpet-blast. As he repeated the line, " When we get to heaven we will part no more," his body began to sway rhythmically to the words, and he spread out his arms toward the people. At the signal the congregation took up the words and chanted them to the monotonous music of one of their simplest hymns, —

> " When we git to heaben, we will part no mo',
> When we git to heaben, we will part no mo'."

The music grew louder, and was accompanied by a gentle rapping of time with the hands and feet and a metrical swaying of the body. The old men and women in the front seats, the church dignitaries seated either side of the preacher, the younger people, who occupied the centre of the church, and the children and lovers, who lurked in the shadow near the door, all joined the chorus, swaying slowly from side to side with dreamy, sensuous faces, —

6

" When we get to heaben, we will part no mo',
   When we get to heaben, we will part no mo'."

Margaret unconsciously lifted her voice and
took up the chant, —

" When we get to heaven, we will part no more."

Her pulse seemed to beat out the measure, and
her lithe body swayed in time with those of the
men and women about her. The music and
the emotion aroused by it seemed to have intox-
icated the dusky crowd ; and it was when this
excitement was at its height that the minister
with a gesture silenced the music he had led
them into.

"My friends, it is good to praise the Lord with
hymns and rejoicings, but it is better to praise
him with your acts. How is the church supported? how is its ministers and its deacons paid ?
By your *acts* of praise. Now the requisite sum
needed for the salary of the elder deacon is fourteen dollars and seventy-five cents, and to-night
I must see that fourteen dollars and seventy-five
cents raised. Come, now, the Lord will help
you ; give bravely, give freely. The money in
your pockets is ready to come out ; give it with
a free hand and a willing heart. Walk up this
way, the brothers are waiting for you."

Four of the deacons, holding baskets in their
hands, stood beside the pastor, and a fifth self-

appointed dignitary taking his ragged hat in his hand held it out for contributions. The people filed down and dropped their money in the baskets, the ragged hat getting quite its share of the offering. The man who held it was of the coarsest African type. His ugly face was disfigured by many scars; but the expression of the creature was so full of a kindly humor that it was impossible to look into it without experiencing a responsive kindliness. The minister's speech had been unusually pure; this fellow spoke with the strongest negro brogue.

"Come, brudder Long, dat nickel is a jumpin' to git out of yer pocket! Step up dis way, young fellahs, step up and help de Lord! Nelly, Nelly, can't *yo'* gib de Lord mor 'n a dime? yo' as gets so big wages — de Lord knows jest what yer gib him to-night, and don't yer forget it. Come up, come up; fill de ole hat. If we make up de fourteen dollars and seventy-five cents, I 'll buy a new hat for de next Sabbath."

His face and manner would have been better suited to a minstrel show than to a prayer-meeting, yet he was so earnest that he moved the people. The old hat was filled twice over with silver; but when the money was counted, it was found to be a dollar and a half short of the requisite sum.

"Take this up," whispered Margaret to a young negro near her ; and the fourteen dollars and seventy-five cents were thus made complete.

"Did you ever see that rascal with the cap before ? " whispered Rondelet.

"No, I think not."

"It's my boy Hero, the greatest scamp I know. That woman with a baby is his sister Leander. They were twins, and the minister who christened them got their names mixed, and the mistake was never corrected. They belonged to my father."

Now that the elder deacon's salary was provided for, the singing began in good earnest. The pastor, whose restraining hand had checked the song just at the generous stage of exaltation, by way of reward gave the rein to his parishioners. The music grew more and more impressive, interrupted as it was by deep groans and excited exclamations. In a pause of the hymn the minister asked, " Where is the miserable sinner ? " He was echoed by Hero, who groaned as if with acute pain.

"Ay ! ay ! Where is he ? Let him speak !"

"Here, here, here ! " was answered from all parts of the church.

"Let him show himself," said the pastor.

" Show yerself, stand up dar ; de Lord sees yer," cried Hero.

Three or four young men and as many women rose to their feet in different parts of the building.

"Oh, my poor sinners, we all have been sinners too, and may be yet again; we will pray for you that the day of grace be not far off."

"Pray for de poor sinners," moaned Hero; "I'se a sinner myself; dis congregation may not see de sin, but de Lord knows it, and de Lord's a helpin' me to wash dis sin away, —

"Oh, wash dis sin from off my soul, wash me !"

The people, always more prone to sing than to listen to prayer, caught up the song, and the rude music silenced the minister's voice, —

"Oh, wash dis sin from off my soul, wash me !"

The minister had no further opportunity to speak, for the singing continued without interruption till the hour came for breaking up. When the benediction was pronounced, a period of social intercourse followed. An old woman with snow-white hair and piercing black eyes offered her hand to Margaret. At this Rondelet interfered, and drew her from the church, silent and full of thought.

As they walked home together through the moonlit streets, Philip told her of his foster-brother Hero, always his friend, once his chattel,

now his servant.   He was a little older than
Philip, and the scars on his ugly black face had
been inflicted by the flames from which he had
saved his master when they were both children.
"We have never been separated, Hero and I,"
said Philip.   "We have seen some hard times
together, but he never would leave me in my
worst straits.   Once while I was ill in Paris
Hero stole money to buy me medicine and
food.   I think he would die for me without
hesitation."

Returning home, they found General Ruysdale
waiting for them on the veranda.   Philip soon
took his leave, and the father and daughter
walked together in the small garden.   "Is not
Rondelet rather a weak man, Margaret?   He
impresses me so."   The General was beginning
to be rather uneasy as day by day Rondelet and
Margaret seemed to grow more and more in
sympathy with each other.   He was suffering
for the first time that jealousy which is not the
least painful one, — the jealousy of a father
regarding a possible lover.

"I hardly know, papa."

"I always have a distrust of men with such
voices."

His daughter answered slowly, "He is very
different from our men, certainly."

"He is a thoroughly good fellow, I believe;

but I wish his voice was not quite so silvery," demurred the General.

" Why," said Margaret, " his most ordinary remark when he speaks to a woman is like a caress."

" I don't know, Margaret ; it does n't seem quite manly to me to be so soft-spoken."

" To treat women as he does ? Oh, papa, I think it is the most manly thing in the world to be gentle to women ! "

She was a little indignant at her father.

" But do you not think him a little weak ? " he persisted.

" Yes, and no. Ninety-nine times out of a hundred he might pass a duty by or shirk a responsibility through indolence ; but there is the stuff of which martyrs are made in Philip Rondelet. He would go to the stake without a tremor for — for — "

" For the sake of the woman he loved ? "

" For conscience' sake ! "

Brave words these, pleasant, one might think, to the ears of any man when pronounced by such a firm, sweet voice, words that might make many a man lift his head high with conscious pride at having inspired the belief they expressed in so true a woman.

Philip Rondelet, passing the rear of the house on his way to Jackson Square, caught their im-

port, paused for a moment, threw away his scarce
lighted cigarette, lifted his hat, as if in salutation,
though the street was empty, and walked on, his
head bowed, his nervous hands idly bending his
light stick.

General Ruysdale was certainly jealous of
Philip. He had confided to Mrs. Harden, to
whose charms he had long since fallen a victim,
his doubts of the wisdom of Margaret's seeing
so much of the handsome doctor. The lady —
Philip's stanch friend and ally — queried why
the same objection could not be urged against
Feuardent. " Robert Feuardent is a child beside Margaret," answered the General. " His
mind is perfectly undeveloped ; he does n't know
the difference between a statue and a bas-relief.
I doubt if he ever heard of Michael Angelo.
He poses for her, and she amuses herself with
him, as she does with that animated plaything,
my rival, General Jackson. The one is quite
as harmless as the other."

" I do not agree with you, sir," replied Mrs.
Harden.

" But, my dear madam, what possible interest
could my daughter and that young creole have
in common ? She knows nothing about horses
beyond their anatomy, and he, pardon me, seems
to know about very little else."

" General, you misjudge young Feuardent. If

I had a daughter, I should consider him a dangerous associate for her."

"My dear Mrs. Harden, you do not know my daughter."

"My very dear General, I know her a great deal better than you do ; and it is my belief that while Margaret knows more of art and is a better sculptor than she has any right to be at her age, it is at the expense of much useful knowledge of men and women. Of their effect upon each other, of character, and of real life she is as ignorant as a child."

Stuart Ruysdale, whose love for his daughter was almost as deep as his pride in her work, was annoyed at what her friend had said. He comforted himself, however, with the belief that Mrs. Harden had failed to understand the girl.

"And even if so," continued Mrs. Harden, somewhat inconsequently, "why not ? Why should n't Margaret fall in love like everybody else ? I don't suppose, General, that you are going to pledge your daughter to single unblessedness ? "

"N-n-no, not that," said the General, doubtfully, prolonging the nasal sound of the n ; " n-not that exactly. I should not wish to influence her in that respect ; but it is a great question in my mind whether she would not be happier to remain as she is."

" I think you are wrong.   It seems to be necessary for women to marry for the full development of their minds.   After thirty an unmarried
woman's brain rarely gets any new creases."
Mrs. Harden spoke with an air of conviction,
and rumpled her pretty yellow hair in a distracting fashion, as was her habit on those rare
occasions when by some accident she fell into
talking seriously, if not sensibly.   " You see,"
she continued, " you can't get something for
nothing.   Of course, men are inferior creatures,
and I quite agree with you in thinking that there
is not one born who is good enough for Margaret.   But what will you have ?   There is certainly more badness than goodness in the world.
If you want to live in the world, the better you
know it the more easily you get along in it.
Men are bad ; argal, to know the world you
must understand men.   You must regard your
future son-in-law " — the General winced — " you
must regard your son-in-law, I say," she repeated
maliciously, " as a sort of necessary evil for the
education of your daughter."

" Your views respecting us men are rather
harsh."

" Of course I am, — at least I mean they are ;
but my practice is *so* different from my views.
I *think* that man is a degree below woman in
evolution, that he is an inferior animal, that

mentally as well as physically he is a less complex and less wonderful being than his mate. I say I think all this quite honestly and seriously ; and yet I avoid my kind invariably, and consort on all occasions with the inferior human male, who, remember, I believe to have been created to do all the disagreeable work in the world for us women, — to keep the streets clean, govern the city, hang the murderers, make the laws, pay the butcher, and fight the battles."

With this exposition of Mrs. Harden's views concerning the sphere of man, the conversation came to an end.

CHAPTER VII.

Rex comes to-day! King Carnival assumes the honors of his brief reign. Work, business, and such cares as may be laid aside at will, are prohibited by the royal and benign mandate. Eat and drink, such of you as have the wherewithal to feast, and be of good cheer, even if your banquet be but a few leaves of lettuce and a handful of golden oranges. Rex has come, and his sway is one of jollity and kindliness to all men. The sun smiles upon his coming, the earth is brave with her earliest spring-flowers, and the mighty river, tawny and swift, is ready to bear the monarch and his crew to the city on its banks. A fleet of ships lie rocking at their anchors. Yachts fluttering dainty pennants, black-hulled merchantmen, ocean-steamers, sloops, and river-boats, and a group of men-of-war, gayest of all in their holiday gear. A revenue-cutter heaves in sight far down the stream, and finally comes to anchor near the flagship. As the cable rattles down through the yellow water, the sparse, clean-rigged vessel suddenly blooms forth into gala attire. In an instant she is hung from stem to stern with streamers and ribbons, gay as the best of them. The cutter is just in time, for a signal-gun now booms forth its warning that the royal procession is about to start. Four and twenty mighty white river-steamers, the escort of the newly-proclaimed king, come slowly round the bend where the city lies in the cool embrace of the Mississippi. The royal vessel is ablaze with jewels and gay uniforms, and as she passes alongside the flagship a salvo of guns blazes out from the sides of the veteran vessel, a shrill pipe sounds, and up the shrouds flash the white-clad sailors to man the yards in honor of the king. High up where the mainmast tapers, stand two youths, with comely faces and locks which catch and keep the sunlight. Festive music fills the air, and hearty cheers echo from war-ship to royal pleasure-barge. The procession moves on, every craft paying its homage to the merry train. The thick gray smoke half shrouds the vessels, and save for the merry music, the friendly cheer for cheer, and the harmless barking of the war-dogs, who open their mouths to greet but not to bite, one might have fancied the great river pageant a sea-battle. General Stuart Ruysdale, standing beside the commander of the flagship, found it hard to realize that this firing and counter-firing was all play. His thought reverted

to that old time still so fresh in the minds of
those who acted in the great drama, and to
reassure himself he repeated the date of the
present year, "18—" "What a difference between then and now!"

"A difference indeed, sir," said a voice at his
elbow.

He turned, and saw a gentleman who had just
paid his respects to the commander of the ship.
He was a gentleman; no one could doubt that for
a moment, though his threadbare coat and dingy
hat were of the fashion of many seasons ago.
He was a tall man, with a keen face, iron-gray
hair, and bright blue eyes; his bearing was brisk,
and had that indefinable trace of the military
which the old soldier never loses. His straight,
spare figure, his square shoulders, his restless,
eager face, showed that his fighting days did not
end with Appomattox. He, like General Ruysdale, was a natural fighter, and life to him would
never cease to be a battle, until the sound of the
final roll-call. He was nearer to forty than to fifty
years, but the deep lines in his face made him
look an older man than he was in reality.

The Admiral introduced the two men: "General Ruysdale, Colonel Lagrange."

"A change indeed, sir," Colonel Lagrange continued, "as I just now heard you observe. Why,
sir, the last time I saw this old ship, it was from

the shore below here, when I tried for three days
to blow her up. I came pretty near doing it, too,
one night; but I can say to-day, sir, that I am
glad I did not succeed. I remember how dark
't was that night,—dark as my pocket ; and I was
creeping out from the shore in an old dory with
a torpedo of my own construction in tow, when a
boat with a Federal officer crossed our bow. He
challenged ; I pulled for dear life. He fired ;
the boats became entangled, and the torpedo
exploded. I was washed on shore and taken up
for dead, with three fingers gone and two ribs
broken. I never knew what became of the other
boat or the Union officer."

"Perhaps I can tell you something of his fate."
It was General Ruysdale who spoke.

"You, sir ! What can you possibly know
about the event ? "

"On the night of the nineteenth of April,
1862 — that was the date of your adventure, was
it not ? — an officer in command of the troops on
board this ship volunteered to make a reconnois-
sance of the line of obstructions which, you remember, was stretched across the river from bank
to bank to bar the channel nearly opposite Fort
Jackson. It was a well-constructed defence of
heavy ships' chains, supported and buoyed by
hulks, rafts, logs, and half a dozen large schoon-
ers. Farragut's fleet, you will remember, moved

up to a point just below Forts Jackson and Philip on the sixteenth of April; and for six days and nights the bombardment was kept up, the cor-vettes and gun-boats taking part by turns in run-ning up, delivering their fire, and dropping down with the current out of range again. The forts replied vigorously. Our object was to force a passage through the floating obstructions, and the officer I have spoken of was returning from his examination of the work already done. He had avoided with some difficulty the fire-rafts which, you will remember, were sent down every night to destroy our ships, and was very close to the vessel, when he saw a boat stealing out from the shore in the same direction. He thought her action suspicious, and gave orders to pursue her. He soon caught up with the crazy old craft, which carried only one man, and challenged her, order-ing the man to surrender. He refused, and bent to his oars. The officer fired his revolver, the man returned the fire; then there was a flash, a crash, an explosion, and the officer knew nothing more till he came to himself the next morning in the sick bay below there. The torpedo intended to blow up the man-of-war had exploded prema-turely. His boat had been blown to splinters, and he himself thrown into the water, from which he was rescued by two of his men, who sup-ported him till relief came from the ship, where a close look-out on his movements had been kept. So the ship was saved, and the only loss sustained was that of the right arm of the officer."

" And his name was ? "

" Stuart Ruysdale, at your service," replied the General, with a salute.

The two men, maimed by the same catastrophe all those years ago, stood looking into each other's faces gravely. To them the river pageant was a shadow; the reality was in the scene they had been living over, in the empty sleeve and worn face of the Northener and the maimed hand and broken fortunes of the Southron.

" It was a terrible mistake," said Lagrange, breaking the painful silence.

" Ay, it was a grievous error. It is those statesmen who involved the whole nation in that bloody brawl, to satisfy their own selfish ambitions, that I hold guilty for all we suffered," returned the General.

" And if you hold them so, what must we, who were broken and beggared by their accursed ambition, think of them ? " the Colonel murmured under his breath.

" I have thought from what I have seen since I have been in the South that the heart of the people could not have been in the scheme of the rebellion. How is this ? "

"It was not until the war had fairly begun ; and then, once in for it, we fought for all we were worth. I was seventeen years old when I enlisted. I did not know — I doubt if a man in our company knew — what we were going to fight for. 'States' rights' was the battle-cry in those earliest days. .My father opposed the secession of Louisiana in the Senate until the last ; and then when his State went, right or wrong, he went with her and took his two sons along with him. Well, well, sir, those times are best forgotten ; but it's strange — is n't it ? — that you and I, blown up by the same gunpowder under the lee of this old ship, should meet aboard of her all these years afterward. She's a solid old hulk yet, and has been done over with new fittings half-a-dozen times since the day she got that rattling fire in her sides. You and I have not fared quite so well, eh ? By Jove, General, it sounds like a romance. Shall we go below and take something to freshen up our memories ? "

They left the deck, the gay company, the cheering sailors, the booming guns, and found their way to the ward-room below.

"I drink your health, sir," said the General, lifting his glass.

"Yours, sir. Let us drink together to the greatest government the world has ever known, the government that I tried, but tried in vain, to upset. May it endure forever!"

"Amen."

It was a solemn toast these two grave elder men were drinking, — a pledge that opened a friendship which was of value to both through the remainder of their lives. A few minutes later, when Margaret, accompanied by Rondelet, came in search of her father, she found him in the company of a very shabby gentleman with a kind face and cheery voice. The two veterans had a map between them, and seemed scarcely pleased at the interruption.

"Is it not time for us to go home, papa?" suggested Margaret.

"My child, I have waited four mortal hours for you. Cannot you wait as many minutes for me?" replied her father.

"The earthworks were two miles below this point, you say," he continued.

"Do you know the Colonel? He is an old friend of mine," said Rondelet. "Let us sit here while they fight their old battles over again."

At this moment Mrs. Darius Harden entered the ward-room. She was a pretty woman, with a pair of bright blue eyes and a mouth that always laughed. It had been said of her that she never went to funerals, because, try as she would, she could not compose her features to a fitting expression of melancholy. She had once said to Margaret, " With such an impossible turned-up nose, my dear, and such a fat pair of cheeks, how *can* I look anything but supremely jolly ? Sweet seriousness is n't my line, and I know too much to try it on." Mrs. Harden bowed to the General, shook hands cordially with Colonel Lagrange, and joined Margaret.

" My *dear*, what a *lovely* gown ! " exclaimed the little woman, seating herself and spreading out her own skirts complacently.

" It 's very nice of you to admire it when you have got such a pretty new dress of your own, Mrs. Harden."

" Such soft, lovely, China-ry stuff as you always manage to find ! Did you ever see such a girl, Mr. Rondelet ? So queer, you know, without meaning to be. I hate original people who pose for it, — if you know what I mean by that sort of thing. Margaret does n't ; she believes she 's like everybody else. Don't you, deary ? "

" No one else can agree with her in that belief, can they, Mrs. Harden ? " said Philip.

" She 's such a mink, — not the animal, you know, but mink, singular of minx. Sly as a little fox. She pretends to work so hard, and then gets all the handsomest men in town to pose for her, and makes them fall in love with her. Now don't protest, Margaret ; I'm sure I don't blame you. I'd do it myself if I could make such pretty things with mud and water and those queer little sticks. So all the women would, though they do talk about your going to the *fête* with Robert Feuardent without any chaperone."

Philip moved uneasily in his chair. What was Mrs. Darius Harden going to say next ? he asked himself.

" They say yours is her last scalp, Philippe le bel. How is it ? Does it still decorate your highly respected head, or does this Atalanta wear it at her belt ? I hope not ; keep it firmly on your pate. I've long had designs on it myself. Do you know that she really is the original Atalanta ? "

" I cannot believe her so hard of heart, Mrs. Harden."

" Oh, can't you, just? Well, you'd better. A flint is tender beside her. I know a secret of hers too. Would n't you like to know it ? Come, what will you give me to tell you ? Now don't say a kiss, like the children, but offer me a good fat bribe, and I will tell you who poses for that lovely girl in her — you know what I mean — her statue — sculpture — that thing she is making out of gray mud."

" The name of the mysterious model ? Name

your own bribe. Shall it be that excursion to the plantation ? "

" I should say so, my brothers. Now for the secret. You must know — "

" Mrs. Harden, you promised ; it would not be fair," interrupted Margaret earnestly, a delicious color stealing into her face.

" My dear, if he had said anything else ; but we all have our price, and for years I have been pining to see the old Rondelet plantation. You shall go too. It 's a dream of a place, and we don't have to start very early in the morning. Train at eight, you know, then steamer up the river, and then — "

" But you have n't told me yet," interrupted Philip, " who the mysterious beauty is. I have a wager about her with Feuardent. We have both been searching the town to find her."

" Well, I have seen her just as she looks in the *thing*, with a little skirt to the knees, the vest, the bow and quivers and buskins, and very little beside. I came to the studio early one morning, and would n't be denied. I rattled the door, bit, kicked, scratched, banged, whanged, and raised particular Ned, till Margaret agreed to let me in — "

" On condition that you should promise never to tell about anything that you saw," interrupted Margaret.

" I know I am a base, a perjured liar ; but then I can't help it, I was born so. The studio door was opened at last ; and when I got in, there was Atalanta, tools in hand, blushing all over, just as she is now, to her very toes and elbows, if we could only see them, and there were two big mirrors, between which she stood and worked and posed, and worked again. Did you ever hear of any one so vain ? She had put her own little self from top to toe in the — the thing ; and you were all stupid idiots not to know it."

" It *is* extraordinary ; for now you have told me, I remember the Atalanta is the image of Miss Ruysdale. But remember that the face is turned away," rejoined Philip, wondering how he could have failed to recognize the lithe strong figure and averted head before him in the fleeting Atalanta of the bas-relief.

" And now that I have betrayed my friend for you, let us arrange the particulars of my bribe. When shall we go ? and can I ever persuade my dear Margaret to forgive this outrage to our friendship and share the fruits of my crime ? "

Miss Ruysdale did not laugh ; a breach of confidence, even in so small a matter, seemed to her too serious a thing to jest about. She was of that rather small class of people to whom there is no satisfaction in betraying a secret or giving a new and startling piece of information. Nine

people out of ten will stifle their conscience and
break faith with themselves for the pleasure of
electrifying an audience with some unsuspected
announcement.   This trait is not altogether an
unamiable one, as it springs from a certain gre-
garious instinct, curiosity and the ministering
to it being the outgrowth or abuse of human
sympathy.

Margaret twisted a slender thread of gold on
her arm, and looked at Rondelet, appealing to
his delicate tact to conjure the chill of con-
straint which had crept over the trio.   Margaret was perhaps a little lacking in the great
quality which is sometimes unwisely yclept a
virtue.   Rondelet possessed it to a remarkable
degree, and the young sculptor had grown to
look to him for the solution of all the knotty
questions of social life which inevitably present
themselves to a stranger in all societies.   Though
he had lived so little of his life in New Orleans, he knew all its traditions and prejudices,
and instinctively divined the differing elements
which composed it and the best way of treating
them.   Mrs. Darius Harden was one of the most
prominent figures of the circle in which she
moved.   She had given the following account
of herself to Margaret : " My father was a Vir-
ginian, my mother a New Yorker.   I was born
in San Francisco, raised in Kentucky, schooled

in Paris, presented to society in London, courted
in St. Petersburg, where Darius Harden followed
me, married in Rome, and settled in New Orleans, where I have lived five years, and which I
alternately love and curse with equal enthusiasm.
For six months in the year I would rather be a
cat in Paris than a princess in Louisiana; for
the other six months I believe that New Orleans
is the only winter city in the world fit for human
beings to live in."

She had the broadness and the superficiality of
those world-citizens who, butterfly-like, suck the
honey from every flower in the world's garden,
while they shirk the wholesome responsibility of
weeding and digging in the patch where their own
particular seed happens to have been planted.
Her female friends asserted confidently that she
had no heart. Most of the men of her acquaintance accepted the theory, and liked her none the
less for believing it. Her genuine good nature,
her hearty comradeship, and her comely person
sufficed to make her an exceedingly agreeable woman; and what right has the world to ask more of
its women or its men? Once that world (which
means you and me, reader, as well as our sisters-
in-law and fathers' wives) is convinced that one
of its people has a heart, it does not rest till it
has endowed that heart with some base or hopeless passion, for which we must either despise or

pity it. Mrs. Darius Harden did well, perhaps, not to wear her possible heart upon her sleeve ; and as long as Darius Harden believed in its existence, it mattered little what other people thought about it. Philip Rondelet shared Darius Harden's belief. Her servants and her dogs would have given their testimony in favor of it, had they been asked.

"Why should we not go to-morrow?" queried Mrs. Harden.

"Why, indeed, if Miss Ruysdale is free."

"Well, Margaret?"

"Thank you, it will not be possible. I am afraid papa will be in despair at my neglected work."

"Now look here, Margaret ; you *shan't* be counted out. I *know* it's because you are mad with me. Now don't be dignified, it's no use. I can bamboozle your father into going — in two twos and a fourteen. General Ruysdale!"

"Yes, Mrs. Harden?" The General looked up from his map.

"I am very anxious to persuade you to join an expedition up the river to-morrow. I want to show you how beautiful the country is there." This with a sudden bewildering smile, a flash of infantine blue eyes, and teeth small and even as the kernels on an ear of young corn.

"Margaret is so disagreeable," continued the wily persecutor. "She says that she cannot spare you, — *you,* who sacrifice so much for her pleasure. It is strange, is it not, that she cannot give up one day for yours?"

"What an ingenious statement of the case," murmured Margaret.

"O woman! marvellous mixture of dove and serpent, how is a poor helpless, clumsy man to resist you?" whispered Rondelet.

"I really am not aware," began the General, looking severely at Margaret, "that my daughter has any authority to refuse invitations in my name. You may count on me to-morrow, my dear madam, as on all other occasions when I may have the good fortune to enjoy the society of so charming a lady as yourself."

"Now you have caught it, my dear little groutiness. Serves you just right," whispered the dove and serpent, pinching Margaret's arm under pretence of arranging her dress. "Get along with you, do, till I persuade the *pater* that it's absolutely necessary that you should go too."

Margaret sighed, blushed, laughed, kissed Mrs. Harden's round red cheek, and followed Rondelet up the companion-way to the deck.

"I wish I had her spirits," she said as she leaned over the taffrail and watched the swift current sweeping onward toward its grave in the great Gulf.

"She wishes she had your talents."

"But she speaks four languages; plays the piano, guitar, banjo, and violin; writes a good letter; and sings in all the languages she understands, and several that she does not. . . . These accomplishments are certainly valued in this community above any possible natural gifts."

"It does not become you, to whom the gods have been so generous, to satirize your less fortunate sisters."

"They haven't been generous. I have worked, and worked, and worked, — that's all. I don't understand *playing* at art. A young girl whom I met yesterday told me she was 'very fond of painting in water-colors; it was such an agreeable pastime.' Pastime! Shades of Fortuny, pastime indeed!"

"It is true that our girls have too many accomplishments, and are little trained to serious work and thought; but that will come in good time, if it is for the best that it should. I like to see you at your work, you are so splendidly in earnest. I always come away from you feeling full of a new strength. You have been a living gospel of work to me, Atalanta. How the name suits you, — Atalanta from the North. You are fit to outrun all competitors in the life-race."

He looked at her and sighed. The old legend of Arcadian Atalanta floated through his mind.

She had been conquered at last. Was he doomed to die in the race for the favor of this Atalanta? Or would Aphrodite help him, as she had aided Milanion of old? His sad face, with its beautiful, tender mouth and eyes, grew firm and strong, as an unspoken determination was made, and Margaret moved uneasily a little farther away from the would-be Milanion, whose gray-blue eyes spoke such unspeakable things. She had been a help to him, with her sober, conscientious work, her simple, earnest endeavor to fill the destiny chosen for her. "She does not know," thought Philip, "that such a career to a woman can only be a consolation. Women should only work when they cannot love. She knows nothing of love, and till she loves can know nothing of life."

"Have I really helped you?" queried Margaret, all the chivalry of her nature thrilling at this admission of her strength and his dependence. To a chivalrous woman — and it seems to-day that chivalry has fled from the world, save when it lingers in some woman's breast — the dependence of a man is a very dear and sacred thing. It is in this chivalrous spirit that many a noble woman sacrifices her life and heart to some selfish weakling, who appreciates the offering as little as he does her who makes it. More often, I believe, does the powerful woman-nature supply, all unguessed, the lacking force of a good but weak man, who with this borrowed strength stands firm and upright in his place, unconscious, as is the rest of the world, of the power that keeps him there. That every woman must find her master is less true than that every woman should find her mate.

Margaret had grown to regard Philip as very dependent upon her, and unconsciously her manner to him had become one of affectionate protection. She had almost lost sight of the quality in him which once had prompted her to say, "There is the stuff of which martyrs are made in Philip Rondelet." And yet, if she had known all the struggles of his daily life, she would not have let the idea slip so easily from her mind. The profession to which Rondelet had been trained was extremely distasteful to him, though he was endowed with unusual ability for it. His father, a well-known surgeon, was conscious of this shrinking from the unsightly details of medical life on the part of his son, and yet was convinced that the rare skill in operation, and the quick, sound judgment in diagnosis which he showed, outweighed his natural aversion to all contact with disease. More from a certain indolent dislike of opposing his father's will than from anything else, Philip had embraced the profession of medicine ; but since the death of that parent, and his return to his native city, he had given up his practice.

From the time he had first met the Ruysdales a great change had come over his quiet, aimless life. The outer room of his little suite had been fitted up, poorly but decently, as an office, and below the window where the flowers grew, a new sign had appeared, bearing the name of Dr. Philip Rondelet in gilt letters. He had procured some hospital work, and was beginning to have a little practice, principally among a class of people whose reward mainly took the shape of thanks and blessings. One woman, whose child he had brought through a painful illness, told him she should pray for him daily. He accepted the prayers, but thought of the colored minister's exhortation about "acts of praise," as distinguished from words.

The pleasant duty of escorting Miss Ruysdale and Mrs. Harden to their respective homes that afternoon fell to the young physician. He accepted Mrs. Harden's invitation to dinner. When they arrived, they found that Mr. Darius Harden was at home. He usually was at home when he was not at his office. The husband of Mrs. Harden was as different from that lady in every respect as the most ardent advocate of the law of opposites could have desired. Mrs. Harden was fair, plump, practical, and jolly;

Mr. Harden was dark, thin, meditative, and romantically inclined. She was loquacity personified; he rarely spoke, save in answer to a question. She was brusque, frank, and communicative; he was a walking handbook of deportment, and mysteriously secretive. She appeared to say everything that came into her head, and, was withal as deep as a well; he weighed his words as if they had been precious stones, and was the most transparent of men. She took life, her husband, men, women, eternity, and the present moment, as a series of jokes; he took his wife, his business, his pleasures, his politics, his gout, his dinner, and the welfare of his immortal soul with the same literal seriousness.

Mrs. Harden never spoke with gravity to her husband; Mr. Harden never jested with his wife. Unobservant people were apt to commiserate one or other of this strongly contrasted pair; but among their intimates their household was quoted as an exceptionally happy one. It was a fashion of Mrs. Harden's — one of those bad fashions which she had picked up in Europe — to speak of her husband as if he were a necessary evil, to be endured on all social occasions. In reality, no party of pleasure was complete to her without the presence of that grave and handsome man.

Dinner was announced; and as Mrs. Harden

passed from the drawing-room she said in an
undertone to Philip: "I suppose Darius will
have to be of the party to-morrow. In this
country, you know, no respectable woman can
stir four steps without her lord and master —
sit here, please, Mr. Rondelet, on my right."
She busied herself in helping the soup. There
was a pause, first broken by the hostess : " Darius
Harden, my husband — "

" Sara Harden, my wife."

" I have been a good and faithful helpmate to
you all these years ? "

" To the best of my belief and knowledge, you
have."

" Then what good or just cause can you show
for not accompanying me to the Rondelet plantation to-morrow ? "

Mr. Harden paused, balanced his soup-spoon
meditatively, as if weighing the matter, swallowed
his *consommé*, and said sententiously : " My dear,
I am very sorry, but to-morrow I am obliged to
attend to some affairs of a very pressing nature."

" Now, Dari, don't try to bluff me. What is
it ? There will be no more business till after
Mardi Gras."

Mr. Harden coughed behind his napkin and
glanced obliquely at Rondelet.

" Now, you old gaberlunzie man, you might
as well tell me first as last."

8

"Indeed, my dear," with an intense look, "there is nothing of any possible interest to you in my engagement to-morrow; it is quite professional, I assure you."

"Gaffer Harden, you're not telling the truth, and you know you're not; and what's more, you know I know you're not."

Mr. Harden shook his head deprecatingly, and said in a soothing voice, "And so Mr. Rondelet and you have at last arranged your expedition. Dear me! I am exceedingly sorry that I—"

"Don't glare at me like a great grinning gargoyle, gaffer. You are a humbug, a regular ringtailed roarer of a humbug. Wild horses, prancing mules, fiery untamed donkeys would n't keep you from going, and you know it. We must take baskets and provisions and wine and things. You will see all about that. We can't drop down upon your dear old uncle, you know, Mr. Rondelet, without any warning, and expect him to bring a table already spread out of the meadow, like little Two Eyes."

"I will make all the arrangements, my dear. I only wish I could be of the party. Perhaps I may be able to arrange—I may even yet—Well, well—I will do my best."

"Gaffer?"

"My dear?"

" Drop it."

And he did.

" Do you know, Mr. Rondelet, that you have not dined here since that night when our dear Ruysdales dined with us for the first time ? " said Mrs. Harden.

" Is it so long ago ? " queried the guest.

" Yes. Don't you remember that you were called away before we had been fifteen minutes at the table ? That was the first I had heard of your having resumed your practice or your title. My husband said at the time that it was always a thing to be remembered in inviting medical men to dine, that they are so apt to be sent for. I don't think you ever told us about the case."

" It was an urgent one, madam, as the messenger said."

" There was such an odd message : something about a lady waiting in the carriage," she continued, entirely ignoring her husband's warning looks. Philip bowed silently, and emptied his glass.

" My dear, it is very warm here. Let us adjourn to the library," said Darius Harden, breaking an awkward pause.

Mrs. Harden rose, and laying her hand on Philip's arm, left the room. At the threshold she gave one significant glance at her husband,

who nodded intelligently, reseated himself, and
lit his cigar.

Passing through the library, Mrs. Harden led
the way to the music-room, — her own especial
sanctum, — and seated herself on a low *causeuse.*
" Sit here, opposite me, where I can see you.'·
She spoke quite seriously, and despite her
turned-up nose and blithe blue eyes she looked
very grave.

" Philippe le bel," she said. addressing him
gently, " Philippe, my good fellow, you are in
need of a friend.   There is no one in this city
that you would trust as you trust me.   Is it not
so ?   And there is no one who has your interest
more unselfishly at heart."

" Dear friend, it is true."

" Then tell me all about it."

" My lips are sealed, madam."

" Professional etiquette ? "

He bowed.

" But if I knew it all ? "

" That would make a difference."

" You know what they are saying about
you ? "

" Something of it."

" That you could tell more than any one else
of the death of Fernand Thoron ? "

Philip nodded slightly, and silently asked per-
mission to light a cigarette.

"That there was an affair," — Rondelet blew a cloud of white vapor from his lips and listened, — "in which your friends say you were but a second; other people — how curiously your eyes have dilated! — other people say that you, you killed him."

Philip inhaled a long breath of smoke, and asked, "And then?"

"And then — hints about some low woman of color. It was this that first made me *know* that it was a lie."

"And why?"

"Because, with such a double sin fresh upon your soul, you would not dare to love Margaret Ruysdale."

For the first time in that strange interview Rondelet changed color. Mrs. Harden continued: "I never do things by halves. Once convinced that you were innocent, I was determined to know who was guilty of the murder — killing, if you like the word better — of Fernand Thoron."

The cigarette was consumed; a heap of yellow ashes in a tray being all that was left of it. Rondelet lighted another with a hand that was not quite steady.

"I think I know who the man is. Will you tell me if I have guessed correctly?"

"I cannot."

"Cannot ! why ? "

"Cannot, because, before God, I am as ignorant of his name as I am innocent of his crime."

" Listen, then."

He bent forward, and she whispered two words in his ear. Rondelet started to his feet with an exclamation. "It cannot be ! " he cried.

" It is," she answered firmly.

At this moment the door was thrown open, and some guests were ushered in, — holiday guests, masked and hooded monks and nuns of the Carnival. When Mrs. Harden turned from greeting them, Philip was no longer in the room.

CHAPTER VIII.

IT was cooler outside than in Mrs. Harden's music-room. Rondelet made his way to Canal Street, which was full of life and motion. The sidewalks, the corners, the doorways and windows of the houses were crowded with people, the steps and railing of the Clay monument black with masses of humanity. From the first stories of the more important buildings temporary balconies had been thrown out ; these were crowded with gayly dressed spectators. Below one of them Philip stopped, and, lost in shadow, stood watching the gay group above him. Fans fluttered, ribbons waved, eyes and jewels sparkled, and the breeze, perfumed as it passed over the garden of fair women, wafted to his ears the mingled sound of light laughter, of jest, of repartee, of whispered protestations, and of answering sighs. Above in the balcony the men and women of the world were taking their pleasure luxuriously ; below in the street the world of men and women were taking theirs, not the least part of which was the spectacle of the

rich toilets and lovely faces of the ladies above
them. Wit, laughter, gayety, a series of gorgeous
pageants, an impassioned pursuit of pleasure, are
what a stranger sees at Carnival time in the
city by the river ; and should one tell him of the
broken fortunes, the life-failures, the apathetic
despair and depression which lie beneath this
brave mask of jollity, he might well be pardoned
for doubting the assertion of the hidden wound,
and preferring to believe in the merry mask and
in the testimony of his own senses. What is
more heroic than a smile that masks a pain ?
And so, bravely hoping for better times, and striving to bring them about, New Orleans in her
poverty, as once in the palmy days of prosperity,
holds high revel at this season of pleasure, and
hospitably opens her gates to friend and to
stranger.

It is a frank and cordial hospitality, that of the
New Orleanists, and one that is not limited to
the rich class alone. There seems little of that
false pride which shuts the door of the poorer
houses because carpets are worn or larders bare.
I have been received in a certain shabby little
house, with sadly worn furniture and absolutely
lacking in *bric-à-brac,* where the gracious cor-
diality of my hosts and the atmosphere of good
breeding and friendliness of the assembled company would have graced a prince's dwelling. It

is not disgraceful, nay, it is not even unfashionable, to be poor in Louisiana.

The sound of approaching music now fell upon Philip's ear, and a pair of mounted officers galloped through the street crying, " Make room for Comus and his merry crew!" A stir of excitement quickens the fluttering of fans and feathers, and the world's people press forward in their anxiety to catch the first glimpse of the great procession. The boys who have been wrestling for money tossed from the tribunes, scramble up the supports, the lamp-posts, the gutters, wherever a foot-hold may be had, and the crowd surges with suppressed excitement. A band of music precedes the pageant. It is the same band that a few days before passed through this street to the strains of a funeral march accentuated by muffled drums. Dusky torch-bearers walk on either side of the vast floats, drawn by richly caparisoned horses, led by ebony grooms. On the cars scenes from the mythology of a great Oriental nation are represented. Here we have the Mongolian Olympus, with its gods and goddesses in superb array, reclining in luxurious attitudes before a superb banquet. A war-scene comes next, spirited and artistic in its grouping. An ice-hell where frosted devils sit among snow and icicles precedes the more familiar hell of fire, where the hoofed and horned demons prod one another with appropriate weapons. The difficult poses are maintained with a grace and spirit which do infinite credit to the actors as the cars jolt along over the rough pavement. A youthful goddess, who might be the spirit of the dawn, casts flowers to the ladies in the balcony, and a red rose falls into Margaret's lap. She bows and smiles, and the youth behind the skilfully painted mask throws a kiss after the rose, while the people in the street laugh and applaud.

"Who can it be?" she asks of the man who stands behind her.

But even if he knows, Robert Feuardent denies all knowledge of the masker. These merry gentlemen keep their identity a secret from the world. The element of mystery adds indeed to the interest of the whole glittering, fantastic parade as it sweeps down Canal Street and through some of the humbler thoroughfares of the town. Not only for the amusement of their peers do these men of the world masquerade in so brilliant a fashion, but for the people, high and low. The procession has passed, and Philip Rondelet follows the wake of the sinuous line of light to its final destination, the Opera-House in the old French quarter. As he reaches the entrance, a carriage stops, and Mrs. Harden, followed by her husband, alights from it.

"How good of you to wait for us!" she cried

vivaciously ; "give me your arm. Dari, have you
my fan and cloak ? "

The wide stairway was lined with flowers and
orange-branches heavy with fruit and blossoms.
Soft many-hued lights diffused their glamour over
the throng of people flooding the Opera-House ;
to-night its dingy paint, its faded finery of twenty
years ago, are forgotten. The music is as stirring,
the company as numerous, the spirits as light,
the women as beautiful, as ever they were in the
old days of prosperity, when the Opera-House
was bright and fresh as paint and paper, tinsel
and brocade, could make it. To the eyes which
are not dazzled by the sight of so much youth
and beauty and jollity, the broken stucco of the
mouldings and the faded, musty cushions of the
chairs may be visible. These eyes (which ought
by good rights to be at home, closed in sober
sleep, and not prying into the mould beneath the
rose) see other things. They see that the frocks
of the fair girls are fashioned of simple fabrics,
many of them bearing unmistakable marks of
home production ; they see that the jewels on the
necks of the matrons are of no great price ; they
see that many a dress-coat is shiny in the seams.
But to Margaret Ruysdale none of these petty
details are evident. She is only aware that she
is in a sea of color and light. From the *loge*
where she sits beside Mrs. Harden, her eyes

wander over the floor where a wonderful congregation of devils and warriors, dragons, fishes,
monsters, knights, and a score of other creatures
of the Carnival are dancing a motley quadrille.

There is a sudden silence, then a murmur of
welcome and admiration runs through the crowd.
Rex with his fair girl-queen has arrived. The
royal pair make their way across the stage to
the *loge*, where seats are prepared for them. The
Queen smiles and bows graciously to the people,
whose loyal love and admiration she cannot fail
to perceive. She is assuredly the fairest queen
that sits upon a throne to-day in all this big
round world. The jewels 'that sparkle amidst her
soft blond curls lose by the contrast ; the rich
satin robe that shrinks back from her shoulder
looks but a poor fabric beside her creamy skin.
Her large blue eyes are full of sunshine, her delicate, transparent face is suffused with blushes.
She is a creature of delight ; not only a carnival
queen, but a queen in the hearts of her friends, a
fairy in her father's house. Her caressing, childish manner, to which the most confirmed woman-
hater yields, is not laid aside with her every-day
dress ; she is to-night a queen of hearts as before,
and the list of her conquests will be swelled on
the morrow by more than one new victim. So
innocently does this fair one win the hearts of
men that I doubt if any man was ever brutal

enough to upbraid her for taking what seems to
have been hers by a divine right which it needs
no Grotius or Puffendorf to maintain.

Margaret is so absorbed in watching the entrance of Rex and Regina that she fails to hear
a knock on the door of the *loge*. Philip answers
it, and the door is thrown open, revealing a gentleman clad in silver and green scales, carrying
over one arm a long spiral tail. He offers the
other arm to Margaret, and she is made to understand by signs that her presence is desired on the
floor. The horrible, grinning countenance of this
demon of the deep is belied by his gentle voice
as he begs the young lady to accept a bracelet,
which he clasps upon her arm, in memory of
Comus. It is a light, delicate affair of no great
value, but to the New England girl its accept-
ance seemed impossible.

" My dear young lady," said the mask, speaking always in French, " remember that you are
not in Massachusetts, but in Louisiana ; and believe me, I am quite old enough to be your
grandfather."

" He may have been a truthful demon," Margaret always said, " but he did not dance like a
grandfather."

It was all very gay and very brilliant ; but the
scene jarred on the nerves of Philip Rondelet,
who, busy with thoughts unsuited to such an

assemblage, soon slipped away unnoticed and took his way home to Jackson Square. The old cathedral, the court-houses, the bronze figure of Jackson on his impossible war-horse were better company to him than that which he had just left. The Pontalba buildings were without sign of life. He lit a match and made his way to his eyry in the roof. As he reached the top floor he thought he saw a figure lying before his door. Bending down, he found it that of a man apparently asleep. Rondelet shook the sleeper and demanded his business. The man opened his eyes, stared about him, and rose slowly to his feet. He was a rough-looking fellow, and Rondelet touched his revolver to see if it was in order.

"What do you want with me?" he asked for a second time. The man nodded; and after fumbling in his pockets, produced a note from the breast of his shirt, which he handed to the Doctor.

"Wait here, and I will see if there is any answer," said Philip.

He entered the room, secured the door, and by the light of the embers on the hearth perused the letter, written in a woman's hand. He read the words carefully, burned the letter, and then, after examining his revolver, left the house in company with the stranger, who was to serve as his guide. They had not far to go. The man stopped before a house in one of the darkest, narrowest streets of the old French quarter. It was a high building of the Spanish time, with light iron balconies at each story, and heavy grated shutters such as the Spaniards love to guard their homes withal.

A woman was standing on the highest of the galleries. She greeted them silently and disappeared. They entered the wide door, and after traversing a long dark passage and crossing a courtyard filled with the heavy perfume of the sweet-olive and the orange-tree, they ascended an open stairway on the outside of the wall which led to an inner balcony. The window was open, and they entered a large bare room where the woman who had signalled them from above stood waiting. For the first time Rondelet saw the face of his guide, and knew it for the face he had seen bending over the grindstone in the little shop. The woman was she who had soothed Therese and begged her to be calm. He understood now to what patient he had been summoned. He heard his name called in a loud, fretful voice from an inner room. The woman pushed him toward an open door, and in a moment he was beside the sick bed. It was Therese. She lay with her splendid hair heaped about, and her bare, beautiful arms twisted above her head. He touched her burning wrist, looked into her

feverish eyes, and questioned the woman who
stood beside the girl. She was the mother of
Therese, and the fellow who had summoned him
was her brother and the girl's uncle. Therese
had been ill for a week, and had sometimes been
out of her mind. That evening she had asked
them to send for Rondelet, and had written the
few words which her uncle had given him.
Therese seemed conscious of his presence, but
since calling his name had given him no sign
of recognition. Rondelet, whose knowledge of
drugs was not confined to those included in the
orthodox *materia medica*, drew from his breast
a small phial; and pouring a few drops into a
glass of water, held it to the girl's lips. She
drank the potion eagerly; and its effects were
soon to be traced in her quieter breathing, the
relaxing of her hands, and the failing of the
fever-flush from her face. The mother, with
that fondness for all medicines characteristic of
her race, asked the name of the potion.

"It is one that you cannot buy," said Philip.
"I learned to prepare it from a wise man of the
East, thousands of miles from here."

The room was large and high, and was
furnished with some taste. The appointments
of the dressing-table, the fineness of the bed-
linen, together with some rare ornaments, were
strangely out of keeping with the appearance of

the poorly dressed man and woman. On the wall above the bed hung a crucifix of exquisite workmanship. The figure of the Christ, carved ' from a single piece of ivory, was yellow with age. The ebony cross showed a crack on one of its arms. It may have been the jewel of an antiquarian's collection filched from a church, for such folk dare to steal even such sacred things ; it may have been the consolation of some sinful sufferer who in the dignity and grace of the dead face found hope and comfort, or it may have ministered to the support of some martyr doomed to die under the torment of the Inquisition of the Holy Catholic Church ; it may have belonged to some cloistered nun, dead to this world and living in that hope of the next which flickers but is not quite extinguished, like the light of a taper in a strong wind. Whoever had fashioned it, whoever had owned it, the crucifix was a gem. To Philip Rondelet, ' a connoisseur in these matters, it had a strange fascination. As he sat beside the sleeping girl, his eyes fixed on the carved image, it seemed to glow with a warm, mellow light from its dark frame ; the bowed head, with its crown of thorns, seemed to lift itself, and the eyes, unclosing, to gaze mournfully into his own. Had Philip belonged to the Church which believes in miracles wrought in the nineteenth

9

century as well as those witnessed in the first, he might have thought that one had been vouchsafed for his own especial benefit. As it was, he shook himself and murmured, " I must have been asleep."

Soon after this, Therese awoke. She recognized Philip, and motioned to the woman to leave the room. When they were alone she said, " I have sent for you because I feared that I might lose my reason and tell things which I may not speak about. You understand me. Do you think that I shall die ? "

" No, Therese, you will not die."

She was silent, and her hand sought some object beneath the pillow.

" I do not want to live, and yet I am afraid to die. I cannot die till I have kept my word."

She grasped the thing that was hidden behind her head, and then asked, " Have you seen Jean since ? "

" Jean ? "

" Yes, Jean Thoron, his brother."

" No."

" Is it true that people say you killed him ? "

Her face contracted with a sudden pain as she said these words, and tears started to her eyes.

" Yes, Therese ; it is whispered, I believe."

" You have not been openly accused ? "

" Not as yet."

" You will not be ; they have been bribed.
But this rumored accusation is the more damn-
able because it cannot be disproved."

" Yes, that is true ; but you must not talk of
these things to-night."

She went on without heeding him : " I *must*
tell you all about it. Listen to me, I shall go mad
if I keep it shut up here any longer. My heart
is bursting ; my brain is seething with it."

She tossed restlessly to the other side of the
bed, and as she did so the object beneath her
pillow slipped to the floor. Rondelet picked it
up. It was a dagger of peculiar design. The
handle, carved from a solid piece of rock crystal,
was studded with rubies and emeralds in an intricate design ; the blade, double-edged and keen,
was stained with a taint of blood. The woman
missed it and held out her hand.

" It is a dangerous weapon for you to handle
so recklessly."

" Give it to me. It was found on him when he
was killed. This stain was made by his blood ;
but it shall be washed out. I have sworn ! "

She kissed the spot and hid the dagger in her
bosom. Rondelet rose to take his leave ; but she
laid her hand upon his arm and besought him
not to leave her till she had told him what he
must know. It is often better to yield than to
resist the freaks of women, of sick women above

all ; and so it was that Philip Rondelet listened
to the story of Therese.   It was told with a passionate eloquence by the fever-stricken girl lying
in her splendid beauty among the pillows, and
the tale was interrupted by bursts of tears and
paroxysms of exhausting anger.   To Philip it
seemed as if scene after scene of a drama was
being enacted before his eyes as he listened to
the torrent of words which poured from her lips.
She told him of the life she first remembered in
Spain, where her childhood had been passed in a
quiet convent, with only the sweet-faced nuns for
company and a score of children of her own age.
Here she grew to womanhood, and here she saw
for the first time the man who had made her life
a reality and no longer a pleasant day-dream.
She had first seen him through the grated window of the convent reception-room as he stood
talking to his sister, her playmate and warmest
friend.   She had known nothing of her home
and nothing of her family, except her father,
who had placed her at the convent, and to
whom she wrote letters at stated intervals under
the direction of the Superior.   Of her friend's
brother, Fernand Thoron, she had often heard,
and soon she heard more and more of him ; for
she had been seen through the grate even as
she had seen through it, and in the presents
and letters which found their way to Fernand's

sister there was always a gift or a word for her
playmate, Therese. She had met him at last,
for convent grates and watchful nuns cannot
baffle lovers' wits, and he had told her that he
loved her, and that when she left the convent
she should be his wife. Then there came a
happy time of blissful, golden cloud-building,
in which all the glorious world seemed to the
lovers to be made but for their pleasure and
their love. All too short this happy time, —
soon to give place to dread reality. A letter
from her lover told her that she must think of
him no more, that he could never see her again.
Soon after this came the news of her father's
death and instructions calling her to the home
which she had never known as hers. The mystery which had hung about her all her life,
and which Fernand Thoron had unravelled, was
then explained. She was no child of princely
blood, no heir to a disputed title ; nothing but
the bastard daughter of an American planter
and of a human chattel whom he had called his
slave. Chance or a remorseless fate threw her
again in the way of Fernand Thoron ; and in that
second meeting the love which had been strong
and pure enough to nerve the man into fleeing from the maiden who could never be his
wife had grown weak and earthly, and they
had yielded to its bliss and to its sin. While

their love was still new and strong, before the
chill of the broken law had blended agony with
joy, a shadow had crossed their path. A man
had striven to put them apart, and in that strife,
Fernand Thoron had yielded up his young life.
Murder, Therese called it, — foul, unnatural
murder ; and under the shadow of that awful
crime Philip Rondelet stood to-day. He should
be exonerated ; he who had cared for Fernand
in his last hours should not be suspected of having caused his death while his murderer lived
free and unchallenged.

What was that man to her or Fernand that
he should have interfered between them ? Philip
asked.

"Nothing to either of them," she answered
hotly ; "nothing but an accursed enemy."

"What was his motive in separating them ?"
he asked.

Her answer was incomprehensible to Philip ;
it was a very storm of words, spoken rapidly in
Spanish, — a language with which he had little
familiarity.

"What was the man's name ?" Philip asked
in a low, grave voice.

Therese, putting her burning lips to his ear,
whispered a name which he had heard once before that evening, the name of a man who called
himself his friend.

CHAPTER IX.

THE rumor had come to Margaret Ruysdale's ears at last, and she believed it. She could hardly have failed to believe it; the chain of circumstantial evidence, to which she could add some links from her own observation, was so strong and so damning. The summons which called Philip Rondelet from Mrs. Harden's dinner-table on the night which people still believed to have preceded the duel, the strange message that a lady was waiting for him in the carriage, his appearance the next day with his wounded arm in a sling, his melancholy, and the apathetic moods she had first known in him, which had now given place to a more hopeful and elastic frame of mind: these things all pointed conclusively to the fact at which people hinted, — that Fernand Thoron had fallen by the hand of Philip Rondelet. It was a great shock to Margaret; and for several days she shut herself from the world and refused to see any one. Then, as hers was one of those natures which instinctively turn to work for their consolation, she betook

herself to her modelling with an impassioned
energy. She had neglected her bas-relief, and
had been living more in other people and less in
herself than ever before. The men and women
by whom she found herself surrounded were
dangerous rivals to her profession. In her Northern home there were no idle people ; and if she
had wished to loiter over the life-path, she would
perforce have done so alone. Here she found
friends, quick-sympathied and warm-hearted, who
had understood her in a week as the old home-
friends had never understood her in a lifetime.
She was conscious that the difference lay not
wholly in the people, but somewhat also in herself. These simpler, warmer-blooded folks, with
their pride, their prejudices, their quick anger,
their quicker remorse, their deadly feuds and
emotional friendships, melted her New England
reserve as the April sun thaws the lingering
frost from the arbutus-roots in the dim Maine
woods. But now the horror at a crime which
to her was not lightened by any sanction of
custom, threw her back upon herself and her
work. Those who spoke about the duel called
it "a most unfortunate accident," "a fatal result
which, happily, did not often attend such an
affair of honor." Men standing in high positions
were pointed out to her as having crossed swords
beneath the great oaks of the duelling-ground in

times gone by. Such affairs were growing rare now, and many, people felt differently about them; but they had their use, no doubt, and society could not be protected without them. Margaret pleaded illness, and for a fortnight saw no visitors and devoted herself to her Atalanta.

What had she felt for Philip Rondelet, she asked herself a hundred times, ere this great horror of him had settled upon her? And then she tried to put him from her mind, and for a time succeeded. With an instinctive knowledge of what was best for herself, — a knowledge all healthy minded people have in time of trouble, — she kept her thoughts and fingers actively employed. When she was not in the studio she was reading to her father, teaching General Jackson, or making fantastic decorations for the quaint little dwelling which thenceforth never quite lost the impress of her fancy. The Atalanta came on famously. It was a composition of a certain merit and of some originality. She had chosen the moment when Milanion, growing weary in the race and hearing the garments of the Arcadian virgin rustling close behind him, turns and throws down the first golden apple. Atalanta pauses, curious, irresolute, and the group of huntsmen and maidens look on, amused spectators of the struggle

between the wily suitor and the light-heeled girl.
The figure of the latter was now complete, and
there only remained that of Milanion to finish.
Robert Feuardent had posed for this figure, and
Margaret was loath to finish it from any less
perfect model than the handsome creole. She
had not seen him since the great ball, when he
appeared early one morning at her studio door.
He had brought her an orange-branch, and
came and stood silently leaning against the
door-post, waiting till she should see him.

He wore the dress in which he posed for
her, — a loose blue flannel shirt rolled away
from the neck, close-fitting nether garments,
and buskins. He must have come at a swift
pace, for his breath was short and his face
and eyes were glowing with exercise. Over his
shoulder he carried the branch of oranges. He
stood in a flood of sunshine, which was colder
than the light in his deep golden-brown eyes,
and he laughed with the glad, free laughter of
a savage child when Margaret turned and saw
him, and started at the sight. He had never
seemed to her so handsome or so winning as
now, when he broke through the quiet gray of
her work-a-day life as a sunbeam breaks through
a dark cloud. A bowl of milk was standing near
her; and taking it silently, she placed it in his
hands and stood looking up at him while he

drained the vessel at a draught. She was a graceful little figure in her straight blue apron, very quiet and demure beside the tropical splendor of the young man who had come to pose for her Milanion. When he had quenched his thirst she welcomed him gravely ; and taking the orange-branch from him, fastened it against the wall.

"You have brought me the golden apples of the Hesperides. I am not ready to model them yet ; they will keep longer than the spirits which make you so fit a subject for my Milanion to-day. It is long since you have been here. Do not tell me of the time or the trouble which has come between ; it is enough you understand that you can serve me only when you are as you are to-day."

His face was a trifle graver after she had said these words ; but he took the familiar attitude, and his identity was soon lost to Margaret as she became absorbed in her work. She wrought long and steadily. The General came and sat beside her, watching the quick skilful moulding of the clay in her hands, — work he would have given all his worldly possessions to be able to do. And later came Mrs. Harden, whom Margaret had not seen since the night of the ball. The excursion to the Rondelet plantation had been postponed indefinitely, and Margaret had managed to avoid Mrs. Harden, as well as

other friends. The little woman seemed annoyed
at finding Feuardent, and after a short visit
took her leave, remarking that Margaret had a
very disagreeable way of being a sort of standing reproach to all idle, harmless people like
herself.

So the morning passed ; and when they had
all lunched together, Feuardent proposed that
they should make an expedition to Lake Pontchartrain, dine there, and come home by moonlight. Margaret objected a little, but was easily
persuaded ; and once in the cars and on the
way, gave herself up to the enjoyment of the
scenery through which they passed. The road
took them through a thick cypress-swamp, where
the water stood in pools under the heavy growth
of palmettoes and marsh-flowers. The death-
moss, running riot everywhere, enwrapped the
skeletons of the trees it had lived upon and
stifled. Soon this dreary place was left behind,
and they emerged upon a broad and pleasant
plain, where a narrow bayou twisted its tortuous
course through a country without sign of habitation save where a negro cabin, surrounded by a
tiny patch of cultivated ground, broke the level
stretch of green. Few pleasure-boats were seen
upon the bayou, but a number of small craft,
laden with fish and vegetables, made their way
toward the city. When the light wind failed

to fill the sails, a black-browed *dago* would leap
ashore, and, lashing himself to the tow-rope, would
trudge along the bank, singing as he went in a
language strange as those rude dialects of Italy
from one of which it is derived. A small boat
filled with oranges floats by, its guardian, a
red-haired mulatto boy, sound asleep, his head
resting upon his cargo of fruit. Far off, the
white-shell carriage-road follows the winding of
the bayou, and between the two thoroughfares
lie stretches of swampy land splendid with the
royal flowers of France. Nowhere in the world
does the flower-de-luce bloom as it does on the
plains about New Orleans, — splendid dark purple masses of it here, and again rows of pure
white lilies, with sometimes a blood-red flower,
and more often one of pale lavender. The land
looks like the royal carpet of the throne of
France, with its thick-sprinkled *fleur-de-lis*, below which, as beneath that splendid tapestry, lurk
many a quagmire and pitfall for the unwary who
would strive to grasp at the · imperial flowers.
And now the bayou widens and comes to an
end, for they have followed it to the lake into
which it flows. On the borders of Pontchartrain
are many cool retreats, where in the pleasant
spring weather, and later in the burning sum-
mer-tide, people come from the city and breathe
the fresh lake-air, plunge into the cool waters, or

ride over the waves in the stanch sailing-craft. Here one may dine pleasantly (and well, if one is an *habitué*) on wide galleries or gardens looking out into the sunset-land beyond the lake. In the gardens are a few very tame wild beasts, and a pelican too well provided with fish and promiscuous victuals to be ever put to the painful extremity in which it is depicted on all the official insignia of Louisiana. Here are alligators, immeasurably old and hideous, which have to be fiercely prodded with long poles, provided for this emergency, to induce them to feed on pieces of raw meat which the unwary visitor pays for.

And all these things Margaret saw and enjoyed a little : but it was not with her as it had been on the day of the *fête;* and Robert knew that this was so, and yet feared to ask the reason of the change. The General followed them about, and examined the ancient fort, whose remains are included in this pleasure-ground. Later, dinner was served, and there was music in the garden ; but Margaret hardly heeded it for listening to a tale Robert Feuardent was telling her of the six tall slim trees which faced each other in a double row within a few yards of the place where they were sitting. These trees mark the graves of six young men of gentle degree who in the old time, when the fort was no pleasure-ground, but a grim war-station, fell to fencing with each other one day for lack of other pastime. The contest, begun in sport, waxed earnest, and finally angry; and when the sun that had seen the six companions in friendly intercourse sank to its grave, it looked upon six ghastly corpses lying on the spot now marked by as many memorial trees.

"Let us come away," cried Margaret, as Feuardent, in a low voice not untouched with awe, finished his narrative. "I will not stay in such an unhallowed place. Why did you bring me here? Why did you tell me this dreadful story? What have you or I to do with murder and death?"

"Who can escape contact with death?" answered Feuardent gloomily. "And why should you shrink from hearing such a story merely because you are a woman? Is it not for you women that these things are done? Strife comes with you wherever you go, and men who have been as brothers become murderers, in deed or in thought, for your sakes. You may not hear a rough word, you grow sick at the sight of blood; and yet the blackest crimes that the heart of man conceives of are committed through your influence, for your sake."

"Is it for women that these things are done, or for the selfish desires of men that are centred in them ?" It was General Ruysdale who spoke.

"I cannot tell," said Margaret, "I think that I know nothing of men ; and if they are as you describe them, I am glad that I do not."

"And why should you hold yourself aloof from sinful men because you, in your ignorance of evil, cannot understand the crimes into which they fall ? If you should learn that your brother or your friend had committed the crime of Cain, which you assume to be an unpardonable one, would not that man still be your brother, your friend ?"

"No; for he would no longer be the man I had loved, but a stranger."

"You would put him from your heart ? You would deny him your love ?"

"He would have killed it with the selfsame blow that sought his brother's life."

The words came slowly, and Feuardent saw that her hands griped each other painfully and that her face was very white and set ; and then without looking at her he read her thoughts, half consciously, as he had done so many times since that day at the *fête* when they had danced that mad dance together ; and when he knew what was in her mind, he started to his feet, stifling a groan that had risen to his lips, and left her without a word.

He came to her the next day, and the next, and every day ; and as the weeks went by, and the Atalanta was almost complete, Margaret's laugh was heard again, though more rarely than before. Her voice had grown a trifle deeper and less like the cool babbling of running water than it had been when Philip Rondelet had first known her. Philip was not there to mark the change, for on the very day after his visit to Therese he had been summoned to his home in the country, where his sister lay desperately ill, and in the life-struggle through which he remained at her side he had no moment to return to New Orleans to seek the girl whose image filled his dreams by day as well as by night. He did not write to her, for the only thing he could have said he had not yet the right to say. Mrs. Harden had left New Orleans when Mardi Gras was past, and there was no one to speak about Rondelet to Margaret, who was putting him more and more from her mind as the days went by. Robert Feuardent, who had been his friend from childhood, never mentioned Philip's name to the young sculptor, and so things went on till the time of the roses was come.

The passage of the seasons in that fair southern land is marked by the blossoming of its flowers. The glory of the roses was over all the city. In the gardens of the great houses the queen

of flowers bloomed sedate and perfect on trellis
and tree ; over the more modest dwellings the
blossoms cast their wonderful beauty ; and from
the neglected garden patches about the hovels
of the poorest denizens of the city, roses, red and
white and yellow, bloomed in a wild luxuriance.
Early in the mornings, before the dew was dry
upon the flower petals, Margaret was wont to
seek a garden where she was privileged to pluck
roses till her thirst for them was satisfied and
her arms became weary with the weight of the
sweet burden ; and here it was that Robert
found her on the very day that Philip Rondelet
came back to the city he had left two months
before.   Here he found her, and here they
walked and talked together among the roses ;
and here Philip saw them as he passed on his
way to Jackson Square, and at the sight of them
turned white and faint, and leaned against the
railing for a minute, and then went on his way
wearily.

CHAPTER X.

ROBERT FEUARDENT had not seen his friend
Philip as he walked in the garden with the woman they both loved, and yet his mind was full
of him that morning. After leaving Margaret,
he took his way to Jackson Square, looking up
as he passed at the windows of his friend's room
to see if there were any sign of his return. All
was as usual. The flowers bloomed serenely
under the shadow of the eaves, and through the
open window he caught the sparkle of the tiny
fountain playing in the aviary. Presently the
sash was raised, and the flowers were watered
by a careful hand. Philip had returned. Instead
of seeking out his old friend, as in other days he
would have done, Robert turned hastily away and
crossed the square. The door of the cathedral
stood ajar, and he saw the priest .at the altar
celebrating the Mass. He entered the sanctuary
and murmured the prayer which had not crossed
his lips for many months. It was a prayer of
words only ; and presently he arose and left the
church with the burden he had brought with him

still upon his conscience. At the porch he stopped
to touch the holy water ; but as he would have
dipped his hand in the vessel, it was struck aside,
and a voice whispered in his ear words at which
his arm dropped by his side, and without a glance
at the veiled woman who had challenged his right
to the sacred water, he hurried from the church.
He had been grievously at fault, and the sin upon
which he had shut his eyes was to-day held up
before him by an accusing conscience which
had slept, alas ! until he found himself confronted
with the man whom he had wronged. His friend
Philip Rondelet had been suspected of a crime
of which he knew him to be innocent, — a crime
of which Rondelet might never have heard had
it not been for himself. For on that night when
the young physician had been summoned to the
deathbed of Fernand Thoron, his own name had
been the guaranty of good faith which had secured Philip's attendance. How had he kept
that good faith ? Philip had not only been suspected of having killed Thoron by the sceptical
gossips of the club-houses, but even by the woman he loved; and Robert, knowing this, had
been silent, and had striven to win her love for
himself while his friend was absent. A grievous
sin, indeed ; and yet he knew in his heart that
had not Philip come back that day, he would
have persisted in it. What would happen now ?

He did not know, he did not care, except for the thought that he might appear a craven in Margaret's eyes. Philip had been too noble to speak, and he had been base enough to hold his peace! Fool that he had been, and worse than fool! So he raved and cursed his folly, and for days together shut himself in his own house and saw no one.

Robert Feuardent was of pure Creole descent. His grandfather, who had come to Louisiana when a child, had married a Frenchwoman, and his father had taken to wife an Andalusian girl. It was from his mother that Robert inherited his beauty; and there was much in his nature that recalled that parent, whom he could barely remember. His father had been a rich man before the war, 'and unlike the majority of his fellow-citizens, had retained a part of his fortune after peace had been established. He had, to be sure, declared himself an enemy of the United States Government, and thus given up all his property in the State of Louisiana to confiscation, and he had received a small document, duly signed by the city marshal, attesting this act of — what shall we call it, devotion, or folly? A little of both, perhaps. To be sure, the only alternative was the oath of allegiance to a government he had given four years of his life and a large portion of his

fortune to overthrow. It was a hard alternative, surely, in that time of bitterness and agony,
happily passed now, and almost forgotten, —
and who shall say that of the two conditions he
did not choose the least humiliating? An estate in Spain, which he inherited from his wife,
made Mr. Feuardent seem still a rich man among
those whose all had been invested in a property
suddenly declared to be no longer Merchandise,
but Man. Robert's father was only lately dead,
and from him the young man had inherited
a house in the older quarter of the city and an
income large enough to allow him to be idle
when he chose. He was known to be in some
way interested in the sugar business ; and though
the interest was a languid one, it kept him linked
with the affairs of the community in which he
dwelt. The young Creole was a person of little education, but of high breeding. For such
training as he had received he was indebted to a
Jesuit college, in which he had learned and forgotten the things which one may learn in such
an institution. He was an authority, however,
on certain subjects to which he had given much
time and thought: No one could guide you to
such good fishing-ground on the edges of Pontchartrain, or in the bend of a quiet bayou, as he
could. He was the best shot among the sports-
men of the place, and was indefatigable in hunt-

ing. He could handle his light sail-boat on the squally, treacherous waters of the lake with that instinctive skill of the natural sailor which can never be acquired. He rode and swam as he danced and sang, because it was in his nature to do so perfectly and without effort. It had been his habit from his early youth to pass several months of each year in a region still inhabited by the remnants of an Indian tribe. At first he had been placed under the care of a missionary priest during these long absences from the city ; but later he had built himself a wigwam near the camp of the friendly red-men, and had lived their life, hunted and fished with them, smoked his pipe in their company, and listened to their traditions and stories.. In his turn he told them of the city and the wonderful things it held. He was known among the tribe as the white brother, and was loved and revered by them as a true and loyal friend. In his trouble his mind turned as it had so often done to his forest friends ; but though he longed for the peace and rest of the woods, he could not leave New Orleans.

Feuardent had already been in love once, twice, perhaps a dozen times in his life, more or less, for his blood was very warm and full of sunshine ; but he had never felt for any woman what he felt for the pale young Northern girl, with her quiet cool eyes, which had once or

twice flashed such fire into his own. The buoy-
ant exaltation which he had known in other
affections was not his now; it was a love that
brought infinite pain and distrust of himself.
He who had always secretly felt a certain supe-
riority over his fellows, masked by a real friendliness and good-will, was now keenly alive to all
his own shortcomings. He had taken to reading books which he found it very difficult to
understand, and fell to talking about those things
which interested Margaret with a lamentable
want of success. He haunted the shops where
prints of the great European works of art were
to be seen. He bought handbooks of art and
cultivated the society of an old school-friend, an
obscure artist little esteemed by him hitherto
on account of his trifling profession and puny
strength. All this to please a girl who called
him a savage, and only cared to see him when he
was in full health and spirits! They had failed
him sadly of late, these irrepressible spirits, and
the heavy arches of his brow were often lifted
into a frown, while the eyes had grown darker
and less full of light and joy than they had been
before this grievous love had come to vex his
heart. He was missed from his wonted haunts,
and one evening a group of friends sought him
out at his house. They would take no denial
from his servant, and finally forced themselves

into the room where he was sitting, despondent
and alone. He greeted them, and asked moodily
what their pleasure was. *He* was their pleasure,
they answered, and a very black-looking pleasure
he was too. Where had he kept himself ? Was
he ill ? Had he lost money ? Did he want to
borrow it ? Was he going into a fit of melan-
cholia ? Was he in love ? Or was he purely
and simply bilious ?

" It 's a case of conscience," said one of the
guests ; " it has suddenly bloomed, late in life,
and Robert is beginning to feel for the first
time the pangs which have tormented my entire
existence. Is n't that about the case, old man ?
I have heard him declare, fellows, a hundred
times, that he did n't know what the word ' conscience ' meant. If he did a wrong thing, he did
it with his eyes open, and took the consequences,
but never regretted it. He looks to me as if
his conscience had struck in."

" No," said another, who was busying himself
with opening the wine which had been brought
in ; " no, it is n't conscience, it 's too much reading. Why, look, this is a dictionary, and here is
a book of poems, — De Musset, *mon Dieu !* and
Shakspeare ! Too much learning has made him
mad. It was high time we came and tracked
him to this unhealthy and unwonted lair of
erudition. Glasses ready ? it' s going to pop."

The last speaker was a young Parisian who had drifted to New Orleans that winter with a portmanteau of faultlessly fitting clothes, a choice selection of the last *bons mots* of the clubs, and the latest slang of the boulevards of Paris. Add to this a handsome but minute figure and face, a complexion snow white and rose red, the title of an old and honorable family, the manners of a prince of the blood, and you have Bouton de Rose, the great social success of the season. He was bright withal and well born, only it was best for him to be out of France for a year or two; and so New Orleans welcomed him with open arms, and repeated his stories, copied the cut of his hair, and tried to sharpen up its French and make it sound like his crisp Parisian dialect. In spite of the efforts of some of the most distinguished of the Creoles, the French of Louisiana has grown flat and broad ; the delicate edge of the language has been blunted by the heavier Saxon tongue with which it is hourly brought in closer contact.

Glasses were filled, and the company drank to the restoration of Feuardent's health and spirits, Bouton de Rose making a speech, gracious and sparkling as the wine he raised to his lips. Robert, confused and shy, said a few words in response, and the conversation soon became general. The contagious merriment of the youthful company and the mellowing influence of the wine soon had its effect on the taciturn host, whose superb physique and inflammable spirits could not long resist the combined influence of good company and good cheer. Music was called for, and Feuardent lifted up his great voice, deep and true as a crystal chime, and sang quaint songs in the Creole dialect. Then he gave them an Indian war-dance and song, which were received with great applause, especially by Bouton de Rose, who promised to make a sensation with the war-dance in Paris when he should return thither. He had just received a letter from that city, and read them all the latest gossip about the new *danseuse* at the Palais Royal and the last *amour* of the *bouffe* actress who was at that time the idol of Paris; who paid for Madame A.'s diamonds, and why Mlle. B.'s marriage was postponed; what the odds were in favor of the American at the Grand Prix; and last of all the latest proclamation of the Nationalists, and what the outlook was for the elections.

A political discussion ensued, under the cover of which Feuardent drew aside one of his guests, Archie Nelson, the artist who had once been his schoolfellow. The host evidently had something on his mind, the utterance of which embarrassed him, for he pulled at his mustache fiercely, and frowned down upon the painter, who waited, wondering what Robert could have to say to him.

"Archie," he said at last, dropping his voice to a whisper, "what do you know about Atalanta?"

"Atlanta? Why, it's the capital of Georgia, man," answered the artist promptly. "Populalation — thousand, founded in — by —, chiefly important from the fact of its being a great railroad centre. It is also widely known from its introduction in a popular Yankee war-song, —

"'So we sang the chorus from Atlanta to the sea.'

The girls are pretty, and the business interests have been looking up lately. That's all I know about the place. Do you think of settling there?"

"No, no; it has n't anything to do with the city," objected Robert; "it's somebody in history, I fancy, some girl who ran races and always won them."

"Female pedestrian, eh? I begin to understand you. Don't happen to remember if she was a Roman lady, or a Sabine girl, or an Amazon?" asked the artist.

"No, but *you* ought to know," said Robert reproachfully. "I have seen her represented in a work of art," he continued. "She carried a bow and arrows, and was very fond of oranges."

" Well, what else ? Is her drapery Roman, or Greek ? Describe her dress, — or does n't she wear any ? " queried Archie.

" Of course she does," responded Robert severely ; " she has on a short skirt to the knee, gaiters, — buskins I believe they call them, — a loose vest, and a wreath of leaves on her head."

" Atalanta — you are sure she is historical ? " asked the painter, rubbing his forehead as if to extract the required knowledge from his cranium by means of friction.

" No, no — no," confessed Robert, " I am not *sure*, but I have that impression. I thought you would know, Archie. What *do* you painter fellows know if you don't know about people in pictures ? It 's your business to know."

The artist was nettled. In all matters of classic and historic lore he had posed with the simple-minded Robert as an authority, though why, as he afterward said to himself, he should be expected to be a peripatetic classical dictionary just because he painted landscapes for a living, was a mystery.

" What are you talking about ? " asked one of the guests. " If Feuardent has been confiding the source of his woes to Archie Nelson, we will get the matter out of him if we have to shake it out by tossing him in a blanket,—won't we, fellows ? "

" No, don't ; it is n't necessary," cried the painter ; " Feuardent 's been giving me an order."

" What subject ? " inquired Bouton de Rose, a connoisseur in pictures and himself something of a painter.

" A nocturne in blue, a study of himself in water-colors as he looked when we came in to-night, to be presented to the Anti-Prohibition Society as an awful warning against teetotalism."

Cards were next proposed ; and the play was growing serious when Bouton de Rose started from the table, threw down his cards, and refused to play any longer. For explanation he turned an empty pocket wrong side out ; and throwing open the window, bade the company look out on the night they were wasting in each other's society. " To find oneself in the company of men on such a night is a crime against the fair sex," he said. The moonlight streamed into the room ; and leaning from the window, Feuardent caught sight of a figure in the courtyard below. It vanished immediately, but not until he had recognized it as that of a woman — a tall woman and a young one, judging by the light step with which she sprang back into the shadow. Bouton de Rose suggested that they should take a stroll together, and the half-dozen companions took their way down toward the levee. The streets were still full of people, although it was very late. They found the levee alive with men unloading a vast cotton-steamer lying at the dock. The whole place was lit up by electric light, and the strong rays showed the dusky workmen as they rolled the heavy cotton bales ashore. Two by two, the men came pushing the great crates before them over the gang-plank to the levee, and darting back again for a new burden. The river, quiet and remorseless in its strength, flowed past steadily and swiftly. Woe to the man who should lose his footing on that slippery plank and fall into the tawny waters ! No possible rescue for him, nothing but a long swooning agony as he would be' swept like a straw down the current, and finally a horrible death by drowning when his little strength should have spent itself in struggling with the mighty waters. The fancy struck Feuardent that the senseless branch whirled along in the swift current at the mercy of the Mississippi might as easily be himself if by chance he should lose his footing and fall just there where the current was strongest. If he should slip and fall, or if some one should push him from behind —

"Come, *mon brave!*" cried Bouton de Rose, clapping him on the shoulder and drawing him back from the edge of the levee, "you are leaning perilously near that devil of a river. You look as if you were about to leap into the flood. Are you asleep, or bewitched? Upon my soul, it looks to me as if a *voudou* spell were on you ; your eyes are starting out of your head! Has some witch willed that you should take a sudden passage to the Gulf *viâ* the river?"

Feuardent laughed uneasily, linked his arm in the young Parisian's, and after lighting a cigarette turned away from the levee. His voice was not heard in the chorus which the young men chanted as they took their way through the deserted business streets of the town, and when the youngest of the party proposed to serenade a lady of wide histrionic reputation then stopping in New Orleans, he begged to be excused on the plea of indisposition.

When he reached his room he poured out a full glass of wine and drank it at a draught. A chill had crept over him ; lighting a fire, he sat beside the hearth, smoking, and staring into the flames with great unseeing eyes. When the morning light began to sift through the shutters, he extinguished the lamp and went to bed.

Then, and not till then, a shadow, which had not been distant from him a hundred feet that whole night, slipped from the courtyard of the house, and with the rising of the sun was gone.

11

CHAPTER XI.

SARA HARDEN on her return to town was genuinely glad to see Margaret Ruysdale again. She had become attached to the lonely young girl who had grown to womanhood without a mother or a sister and with next to no feminine influence in her life, her father and his friends having always been her most intimate associates. It was to this fact that Sara Harden attributed the serious character of her friend. "If I ever have a daughter," she had said, "I shall bring her up just as Margaret has been brought up. She shall never speak to a woman if I can help it. Women make one another silly. We drop in to see each other, and spend the morning wasting each other's time in talking gossip and ball-dresses, servants and teething-babies. We don't dare to talk to men like that; they would n't stand it. We discuss things worth thinking about with them. But with our sisters we feel bound to limit ourselves to the useful sphere of domesticity, and it does n't do us any good. Do you think I would use white

sugar instead of brown to put up my sweet-
pickles, because every time I see my next-door
neighbor she advises me to do so, and has ad-
vised me to for the last five years? In house-
keeping, as in every other matter in life, you
can only learn by burning your fingers. I think
women were never meant to associate with each
other. They are too narrow; and they go on
making each other smaller and smaller, instead
of getting broader and strongèr by contact with
great coarse-grained men. Go to! I do not
consider them advantageous or proper associates. I might have amounted to something
myself if I had n't been blighted early in life
by five sisters and four aunts."

"But Sara," objected her friend, "see how
differently men treat you! They all fall in love
with you, and you can twist them around your
little finger, — even papa. You can make him
do whatever you like. I don't know how to
manage them at all, though I have lived among
them all my life. It's a penalty you would not
like to pay to have men treat you as if you were
one of themselves."

"O thou littlest humbug! How about certain young Creoles with big eyes, not to mention
my own ewe-lamb Philip, which thou hast calmly
taken from me without even a 'by your leave'?
Lies, all lies!"

Margaret had passed her childhood and early youth in Woodbridge, the quiet New England town where the Ruysdales had lived, father and son, ever since the old original Ruysdale left the Dutch colony of Manhattan and took to himself a daughter of the Puritans, a century and a half ago. When Margaret was barely sixteen her father had taken her to Europe, where, for the next four years of her life, she had devoted herself — it would be nearer the truth to say that she had been devoted — to her art. Her artistic education had begun when she was scarcely out of her babyhood. She had worked so arduously that there had been little time in her life for society ; and so it had come about that though she had been thrown almost exclusively with men, her relations with them had had little personality. Flirtation — that rock on which many an American girl's heart and life are splintered into a myriad pieces — was known to her by observation only. The hours and years, the talents and force, which so many of our young girls evaporate in that futile and unsatisfactory pursuit, had been devoted by Margaret to her art. It is not likely that this singleness of purpose could have developed itself so early in her had it not been for the strong influence of her father, who had wellnigh absorbed her life in his own. He had treated her, ever since she could remember, as his comrade and equal, talking and reading with her on the subjects which interested him, and on which he willed that she should concentrate her own powers of thought. He had thus robbed his child of her childhood, — a grave error, and not an uncommon one with fathers. A boy's boyhood is too vigorous a thing to be balked of its bent ; but the nature of a little girl is a wonderfully pliable and soft material, out of which a self-centred man may easily shape a careful child-woman for his companion. Margaret had not been ·without suitors, for the comfortable fortune she had inherited from her mother had more than once given her the opportunity of making an advantageous European match. She had not been without admirers, for her charm of manner, her grace, her fresh sweet face, and her lithe strong figure were attractions which had not failed to make themselves felt. But of lovers she was as ignorant as of the inhabitants of Mars. She knew quite well how to make men welcome at her father's table, how to put them at their ease if they happened to be shy, how to make her drawing-room pleasant and homelike to the homeless ones ; but here her knowledge of them stopped.

Mrs. Sara Harden was in all respects the opposite of her young friend, and had borne the reputation of being a flirt of the most dangerous character before her marriage. Since that time she had somewhat kept up the appearance of the same thing with men whose relations to her were of the most innocent and friendly nature. It was another of those bad European notions of hers, that a woman must have many admirers if she desires to keep alive her husband's devotion to her. They interested each other, Margaret and Mrs. Harden, because their lives and experiences had been so entirely unlike; and so they kissed at meeting after Mrs. Harden's long absence, and the kiss, so often a foolish form between women, expressed a cordial good-will and pleasure at seeing one another again. Margaret and her father had come to Mrs. Harden's house and had found that good lady sitting in her garden, watching a game of lawn-tennis between her husband and Robert Feuardent.

"We are very glad you have come back, Mrs. Harden, for we are thinking of flitting northward in these days, — are we not, Margaret?" said the General, watching his daughter as he spoke.

"Are we, papa?" Margaret answered, with an unsuccessful effort to appear indifferent. "I did not know it. I should be sorry to go just now; it is so beautiful here."

"Yes; but the intense heat may begin any

day, may it not, Mrs. Harden? Look at that flock of cranes flying northwards. Should we not take warning by them?"

Margaret looked in the direction indicated by her father. A vast letter V was outlined in the sky by a flight of cranes, which looked as small from their great distance as those on a Japanese fan, although their curious harsh cry was distinctly audible.

"No, it will not be hot for some time to come," said Mrs. Harden, "it will be as it is to-day for a month longer; you must not think of leaving us just yet, General." This with a tender, deprecating smile, which warmed up the harmless vanity of the unwary General to a melting-point.

The game of tennis being ended, Robert Feuardent leaped over the net, and, racket in hand, seated himself at Margaret's feet at a little distance from the others. He had denied himself the sight of her since that morning in the garden, through some idea of atonement to Philip. All the glad blood rushed to his face as he looked into her eyes and saw that she was still friendly and glad to see him.

"When may I come again to you? It is a lifetime since I have seen you. I have missed you so terribly. Do you know what it is to miss a person as I have missed you?" he said.

"How can I tell? I have certainly wanted to

see you very much. I have not done any work
while you have stayed away, and now my father
speaks of going home; I fear I shall never finish
my Milanion."

"You only wanted your model, then ; you did
not care to see me ? "

"But you *are* my model."

"Yes, and something else besides. Shall I
tell you what ? "

The twilight had fallen on them, and through
the open door of the drawing-room streamed a
bright light, showing the face of a man who at
that moment advanced toward Mrs. Harden. It
was Philip Rondelet.

"I am so glad you have come, Dr. Rondelet,"
said Sara, rising to greet him ; "I have been
wanting to see you ever since my return. Here
are some friends of yours, — Margaret, Mr. Feuardent. General Ruysdale and Darius have just
gone inside."

Margaret, grown white and trembling, rose,
and in the dimness either did not or feigned not
to see the hand Philip held out to her. Bowing
slightly to Feuardent, he took his place at Mrs.
Harden's side.

"You have seen Miss Ruysdale, of course,
since you got back," she whispered.

"I have not had the good fortune to find her
at home," answered Philip.

"And has this sort of thing been going on?"

"Evidently."

"And you have not spoken?" said Mrs. Harden. "You carry your Quixotic ideas too far. ·Thank Heaven! I am a woman, and will not sit still and see a crying shame like this. Honor! I believe in honor only where it is due."

"There would be little of it in the world, madam," answered Philip, "if we all felt as you say you do."

"Shall we go inside? This is more than flesh and blood can endure. I am going to insult that man in my own house, — a thing I have never done in all my life before."

Mrs. Harden rose, and with a heightened color and in freezing tones said, "Mr. Feuardent, you will excuse me, I am sure; but these friends of mine are going to do me the honor of dining with me, and as we are going out afterward —"

"Madam," said Robert, starting to his feet, "it is I who should apologize for intruding so long upon your hospitality. I wish you good evening."

He was gone, and Sara Harden was left to get through her dinner-party as best she could. "It was not what might be called a cheering repast," as Mrs. Harden afterward remarked to her husband, "with Margaret as stiff and cool as one of her own marbles, and Philip all good manners, and his eyes flashing like blue-steel cimeters. But we got through it somehow, thank Janus! Good-breeding is a bridge that can span the most fearful social chasms. Your rich vulgarian thinks he can afford to laugh at it. Bah! it's a virtue which I have sometimes seen rise to the height of heroism."

Robert Feuardent strode down Esplanade Street flushed and angry, with a sick, choking feeling in his throat which grew and grew as he gradually left his resentment behind him. He had not failed to see Margaret's slight of Philip Rondelet, his life-long friend, and he knew that he was responsible for the misapprehension under which the young girl had acted. The sting of Mrs. Harden's hardly veiled insult was soon forgotten in the pain of a deeper wound. He took his way to the garden where he had so often walked with Margaret; and seeking a dark corner, flung himself upon the grass among the flowers. His great form trembled with passion, and at last a sob broke from his lips, a torrent of tears and sighs burst from his overburdened heart and were lost in the murmuring grass. Tears, welcome and rest-giving to women, scorch and sear the eyes of men like drops of molten metal.

Robert Feuardent, lying writhing in the dark corner, with clenched hands striking at his breast, his head, the senseless earth beneath him, suffered mortally as the hot drops sprang from his eyes. In his agony he called upon the name of a man who had been dead many weeks, with a passionate remorse and tenderness ; and mingled with these scarce intelligible words of entreaty was his own father's name and that of some woman spoken harshly and reproachfully. It was a grievous sight, this strong man laid low in his pride of youth and beauty, a sight which would have touched the heart of any of God's creatures capable of pity ; but in the woman who had followed him, and was now standing near by hidden in the shrubbery, there was no pity, only a savage exultation at his pain. She too called upon the name of a dead man in whispered tones, — the name of her dead lover ; but it was with a cruel glee that she conjured him to look from his grave and see her vengeance. The young man rose to his knees now, and prayed aloud that he might die, that the burden of sorrow might be lifted from him ; he could not bear it longer. His own sin, the sin of him to whom he owed his life, the sins of that lost woman, — all were weighing upon him and pressing him down, down into a depth of despair blacker than any hell !

"Fernand, the time has come for me to strike!" whispered the hidden witness of his agony; and with the spring of a tigress she was upon him as he raised his hands above his head, dumbly asking for comfort. She caught him by the throat, and he saw the gleam of a knife flashing between himself and the moonlight. Before she could strike, the weapon was wrenched from her hand and sent whirling into the shrubbery. He held her for a moment closely pinioned, looking down into her white face, which had lost all trace of womanhood in its look of rage and baffled desire. When he spoke at last, it was in a low voice, more sorrowful than angry, —

"Therese, has there not been enough shame and sin and blood between us two without this? Remember who it is that you would kill, and thank your God that you were spared this crime."

She struggled to undo his hands, but he held her firmly.

"You must listen to what I have to tell you. I have money for you when you need it, and I think you need it now. I will send you back to Spain, to your convent, or where you will. There is nothing for you in this country but more sin, more shame, more madness; for I believe that you *are* mad to-night. Go back to the land where you have friends, — friends who never need suspect who and what you are. Do you know that I could imprison you for your whole miserable life for what you have tried to do to-night ; that if others had seen your act I could not have saved you from the living death of a jail?"

" Let me go," she muttered ; " you need not fear, I have no other weapon."

He freed her hands.

" Now listen to me," she continued. " I will never leave this place while I can injure you. I have an account to settle with you that is of longer standing than either of our lives, and I believe that I shall live to pay it. Wrong for wrong, blood for blood! I have sworn it."

She stood for a moment motionless in the moonlight, one arm lifted above her head like the figure of an avenging fury ; and then fled from him into the darkness.

He stood where she had left him, thinking deeply for some minutes. His brain, which just now had seemed on fire, had grown clear, and he thought with an intensity which only comes in moments of great excitement. His pulses, which had throbbed so violently, had slackened, and the fever of mind and body was gone, chilled by the cold glint of that jewelled dagger which had gleamed so close to him. The passion had gone

out of him, and there remained only a cold sense
of a danger averted for the moment, but still
hanging over him.   Therese had meant to kill
him, still meant to do so.   Life, which a half hour
ago had seemed so hard a thing, now looked full
of golden possibilities, of sweet realities.   The
world which held Margaret Ruysdale was dearer
to him than any heaven of angels.   He would
not die ; he would baffle that mad creature who
had sworn to take his life, and send her away
beyond reach of him.   Yet how could he accomplish this ?   It is not more difficult to chain
running water than to balk a wilful woman of
her way.   The bond between this wretched creature and himself still held him, though she had
lifted her hand against him murderously.   He
could not give her over to the officers of the
law.   If she had succeeded, if that sharp steel
had found his heart, what would Margaret have
felt, — Margaret, whom he had left so pale
and still in the moonlight with Philip Rondelet ;
Philip, his friend, the man he had wronged so
grievously ?   If he had died without speaking,
Margaret might never have known that Philip
was innocent ; Philip would never know how
grievously he had repented his breach of faith !
It was but a chance that had saved him.   Another time he might not escape so fortunately.
He struck his hands together at the thought

and said aloud, " Now, while there is yet time, I
must speak ; " and so passed out of the garden
with a slow step and a quiet, pale face.

At the Darius Hardens', dinner had been got
through with somehow, General Ruysdale and
his host bearing the burden of the conversation.
The two ladies had retired as early as possible to
the music-room, where they were soon joined by
Philip, who came to take leave. Mrs. Harden
was at the piano singing the last comic air from
the "Folies Bergères " which Bouton de Rose had
taught her, and Margaret was standing at the
open window pulling the ears of Mrs. Harden's
skye-terrier. Philip was about to leave, but Mrs.
Harden asked him to turn the pages of her song ;
and he lingered, not unwilling to be longer in the
company of one who, gentle or unkind, was always
dear to him. It was pleasant to look at her even
while she kept her head so obstinately turned
away from him. The twist of soft hair, the
curve of her white neck, the slim waist, and delicate outline against the darkness of the open
window, were only less beautiful in his sight
than her deep eyes and small flower mouth. He
was glad that other people found Margaret only
" rather pretty," or " sweet-looking ; " to him she
had a wonderful loveliness, — a loveliness which
was not apparent to the first glance of any careless observer, but which grew and grew as one

learned the graceful play of her movements, the infinite changefulness of her expression.

To these three people came Robert Feuardent unannounced. The curtain of the door was pushed gently aside, and he who had left them flushed and excited, in haste and resentment, had come back white, quiet, and full of that strange awe which falls upon those who have escaped a great calamity.

Mrs. Harden arose and came to meet him, saying, "What has happened to you? You look so strangely — Philip, a glass of wine." And the pale girl at the window turned and looked at him, and twisted the dog's ears till it howled and licked her hand deprecatingly.

"Thank you, I am quite well, — or shall be soon," said Robert, in a voice that would not be quite firm. "I have come to speak to you, Philip, and it is well that these two witnesses are here to listen to what I have to say. I have done you a great wrong, — a wrong that I have come to set right." He paused a moment and looked at Margaret, as if to gain courage from her face. "On the thirteenth day of December, four months ago this very night, you were summoned from this house hastily and peremptorily. The message brought you was an unusual one, and aroused comment at the time. The next day the world knew that a man," — his lips trembled and his voice came so low that the two women moved nearer to him and Rondelet watched the motion of his lips, — " Fernand Thoron, had died suddenly. After a time it was whispered that he had been killed in an affair of " — he hesitated — " in a duel; and again it was breathed that Philip Rondelet knew more of his death than any other man, save the dead man's brother and the physician who had been present, both of whom had left the country immediately after the affair. Then it gradually grew to be believed that the man had fallen by Philip's hand. This came to my ears many weeks ago ; and I, who alone knew the truth, kept silent." He paused, as if for want of breath, and there followed a moment of silence, which seemed to his hearers of unendurable length. At last he went on : " I said to myself that I did not speak because the dead man's secret must be kept and the honor of another person whom I was bound to protect, spared. I know now that I lied to myself ; that I was silent for fear that the blame should rest where it belonged, — upon the miserable head of the man who had killed one friend and was now betraying another." He looked now at Margaret only ; with mournful, pleading eyes he spoke to her alone in a low, broken voice: " I kept silence ; but the time has come for me to speak, to declare that Philip Rondelet came only to ease Fernand Thoron's dying hours. The man who killed him, the man who has so long been a false friend, stands before you; deal with him as gently as you can."

There was another space of quiet. Margaret, with her hands clasped above her heart, stood silent, looking down, and Philip, with a troubled face, watched her every movement. She had given one low cry; but whether it was a cry of grief or of joy, he did not know. Mrs. Harden wept silently, and the terrier rubbed himself sympathetically against her slipper.

The self-accused man stood silently looking into the faces of his three judges. For a moment no one moved or spoke; then Philip took his old friend by the hand, and Robert, flinging his arms about him, kissed him on either cheek. Together they left the room, and through the open window Margaret saw them walking arm in arm down Esplanade Street. For a moment everything between the two men was forgotten, save the old affection which had revived at the hand-touch. The jealousy, the suspicion, the wrong inflicted, the wrong endured, were all put aside, and they were as brothers. In the generous emotions of atonement and forgiveness, the deadly wound their friendship had received seemed to be healed. To-night they both believed that not even a scar remained.

To-morrow's reflection might show each that a broken friendship, no matter how closely riveted it may be by remorse and forgiveness, can never again be the flawless whole that it was before. The mended vessel will do very well in this life of cemented affections, but it can never ring clear again like the perfect crystal vase of an unbroken trust.

Margaret watched Philip and Feuardent as long as she could see them from the window, and then turned and looked at Mrs. Harden, whose blue eyes had grown very dim with tears. The young girl was dry-eyed and silent.

" Margaret, you look so bewildered ; did n't you understand it all ? " said Mrs Harden, with a little sob.

" Yes, I think I understand," answered Margaret.

" What a cold, heartless thing you are," Mrs. Harden continued, " to see those two beautiful dears standing there, like two knights-errant of old, just adoring you, and telling you so with eyes plainer than I am speaking now, — and you like a little prudish statue without a word or look or blush for either of them. I don't believe you have got any heart at all, — indeed I don't."

" I don't know, dear ; perhaps I have not," answered Margaret, her hands still tightly pressed to the spot where the organ whose existence her friend denied is usually supposed to have its place.

"I am sure I don't know which one loves you the best! And then their reconciliation, — just like Damon and Pythias, you know; only I forget if they ever quarrelled. I knew it all the time, so did Philip, that Feuardent had shot young Thoron; and yet Philip never said one word to clear himself. I call it angelic of him; and his face when he stretched out his hand to Robert was just like a saint out of heaven giving his forgiveness and blessing to an erring sinner."

Margaret nodded, and picked up the dog again.

Mrs. Harden went on : "As to Robert Feuardent, I never liked him half so well before in my life; he was so splendidly unsparing in his self-denunciation that he made one feel he had n't been so very bad after all. How handsome and black he looked, — just like Erebus, or Pluto, or some of those dark creatures. I wonder what they fought about. There was a woman mixed up in it somehow — an anomalous creature who some people insist is a lady, while others declare that she is a vulgar colored woman. *I* don't believe she was on the other side of Colorado, as we call it; Feuardent never could have stooped so low. But I must n't talk about such things before your innocence; forgive me! Tell me, Margaret, which do you like the best ? You have n't any business to let them both go on loving you so, — it 's really immoral."

Margaret smiled a little absently, and began to braid the long hair on the skye's forehead.

" Don't do that ; he can't bear the light in his eyes," said Mrs. Harden.

Margaret put the dog down, and took up a skein of wool to wind.

" You are spoiling my best iced worsted ; don't wind it so tight. I never saw such a girl ; you are really nervous, I believe, and want to keep your hands busy at something, no matter how disastrous the results may be."

Margaret threw the skein back into the work-basket, and going to the piano played a few bars of a waltz. It was the music to which she had danced with Robert Feuardent on the day of the *fête.* As soon as she recognized it, she struck a few chords of a new galop, and then closed the instrument, and went and looked at herself in the glass ; she unclasped her necklace, and twisted it twice about her arm.

" Does n't that make a pretty bracelet, Sara ? "

" Oh, yes, of course," answered that lady pettishly, " and the hand is still prettier. I suppose that 's what you want me to say. Which of them shall you bestow it on ? I *must* know."

"And if neither of them has asked for it, how shall I answer you?"

"But you know."

"I don't know. I know nothing about love, about men, about women, about myself even. It was terrible for me to believe that Philip Rondelet was a murderer, the hero of an ignoble intrigue, he seemed so refined, so pure-minded; but it is almost worse to find that Robert Feuardent's frank face and simple manner should mask a libertine and a Cain. I have seen too much of your men. I have gone below the surface of good manners and courtliness, and have found vice a thousand times uglier because it lies beneath so pleasant an exterior."

"Ah, my dear, you take these things too seriously. Men are the same all the world over,— north and south, east and west," Mrs. Harden commented.

"Then no more of them for me! Better, far better, the old quiet, colorless life."

"That can never come back to you, Margaret. It is past, even as your childhood is past. You can never be a child again; you can never go back to your marbles and be satisfied. The shadow of love is upon you, and life will never be the same to you again, my poor child."

The elder woman spoke seriously and gently, as Margaret had never heard her speak before, as she touched the young girl's forehead with her lips. Then Margaret lost her composure, the tears trembled to her eyes, and the two women wept together; but whether Margaret's tears flowed for Philip Rondelet or for Robert Feu-ardent, her friend could not tell. It may be that she herself did not know; for to an untried heart love and friendship often masquerade each in the other's shape.

CHAPTER XII.

"Was Margaret glad, or sorry, that the cloud which hung over him had been dissipated?" Philip asked himself a thousand times; and at each self-interrogation he either felt his heart grow sick and faint with doubt, or quicken its beating with the joy of hope. There was something so sacred to him about this young girl's heart that he dared not ask her to lift the veil which hung about it and to unfold to him its virgin sanctuary. He silently offered up at that white shrine a love as pure as ever man was blessed with. He loved her as no man should ever love her again, with a love surpassing the love of self. He thanked God for that love, and was glad to think that so great a wealth of affection was his to lay reverently at her feet. Should she take it or leave it, he was always the richer for having it to give; and so he spoke only with his eyes and voice, which grew tender when she was near. Human lives have their ebb and flow, their storms and calms; and in the days which followed Feuardent's confession there was peace and quiet for Philip. He saw Margaret very often. He sat with her while she worked in the afternoon, when his own day's toil was over; and in the sunset-hour they lingered in the little garden, where the splendid rose-bloom wrapped the modest little house with its sweetness. Up and down the narrow paths they paced, her loosened hair sometimes touching him as if with the touch of fire. She was not quite what she had been to him in those early winter-days. The perfect frankness of girlhood had left her, and the reserve of young womanhood had insensibly taken its place. She talked to him of her work as of old, and in odd moments modelled for him a little statuette of herself in her long blue apron. It seemed as if she wished to turn to him the artist-side of her nature, which he could understand, perhaps, better than any one else. He carried the little figure home and fashioned for it a shrine, carved with more love than skill. She learned from him about his poor patients, and the hospital where he labored was often brightened by her presence. He was conscious that she tried to atone to him for the injustice she had done him; but from the night when she had learned the truth, they never spoke of the past or mentioned Feuardent's name. The melancholy which at first had hung about her grew less perceptible, and the smile which had seemed forced at his coming, now lighted up her earnest face naturally.

It was in these days that the long-planned excursion to the Rondelet plantation came off. The party assembled in the early morning at the levee, where a small steamer chartered for the occasion awaited them. The Hardens were the first to arrive ; and shortly after, Bouton de Rose drove up at a sharp pace in a very shabby cab, from which he descended "with the royal air of a prince of the blood leaving his chariot of state," as Mrs. Harden said. Colonel Lagrange, very much buttoned up and military in his appearance, came next ; and last of all the Ruysdales with Rondelet, who had gone to fetch them.

The day was an exquisite one, and the guests seemed to be in the best of spirits as they stepped on board the steamer. Mrs. Harden's face was wreathed with smiles, and her light, merry voice rang out cheerfully as she took an affecting farewell of her skye, yelping in the arms of the black coachman.

"My dog," she said, "my dear dog, I cannot take you with me ! I dare not risk your precious life on the treacherous billow. Poor forsaken one, try to be cheerful, and don't chew up the new sofa-cushion while I am away ! The old ones are still quite good enough for you to spoil.

Sneeze, my idol, farewell! I shall not be happy till I again fold you to my heart. Dari,"—turning suddenly to her husband, and speaking in an undertone, — "do you think Mary remembered to put in my curling-tongs and prayer-book? I can't go without them."

"The tongs are there; I saw her put them in," said her husband.

"Well, that's the most important; I suppose I *can* pray without my prayer-book, though I could not have curled my hair without my tongs. Good-by, my deserted love! farewell, my own little Sneeze!"

The laugh which followed Mrs. Harden's touching leave-taking of her skye was very irritating to one person who heard it. Not to the stevedores at work in the mammoth ship near by, surely, nor to the group of idlers who were watching the departure, but to a man standing behind a pile of cotton-bales, whose eyes were fixed on the face of the young girl about whose comfort Philip Rondelet was busying himself. The physician placed a stool beneath her feet and brought a cushion for her back; and at these very simple acts of courtesy the unreasonable being behind the cotton-bales ground his teeth, and, I regret to say, swore roundly, cursing the steamer, the footstool, the Rondelet plantation, and everybody on the boat, always excepting the young lady who leaned comfortably back in the camp-chair, quite unconscious of the maledictions called down upon the devoted heads of her companions.

The people on the steamer, after watching the preparations for departure, settled themselves to enjoy the sail up the river. They passed great orange-groves, where the flat monotony of the landscape was agreeably broken by masses of dark foliage. Groups of pecan-trees, tall and beautiful in shape and color, were outlined against the crystalline sky. Here and there a few scattered negro cabins were to be seen; but for the most part there was little sign of habitation on either bank. At one point they passed an enormous raft of logs brought to anchor at the river-bank. Margaret was much interested in this, which was to her a novel sight. "I wish I could see what it is like to be on such a raft," she said, "and what sort of people live in that queer little house."

Philip, who knew no better law than Margaret's wish, gave the necessary orders, and five minutes later she stepped lightly on the outermost of the great trees solidly chained together. A man came out of the shanty set in the middle of the raft and asked if they were come to buy his lumber. He was a rough-looking old fellow, hard of face and voice. When Margaret told him that she had never seen such a raft before, he made her welcome to his drifting home. "'U'd ask you to step inside, on'y the boys is thar — taint much of a place for ladies, but good 'nuff for we 'uns. That's my youngest cub; he was born on a raft, and larnt all he knows on one. Yes, we come from Red River; been three months on this yer raft oo' logs — fair lumber too, as ever growed."

The cub was an uncouth creature, too tall for his trousers and sleeves, too short for his boots and coat. He stared at Margaret, and presently set to work building a fire in front of the door of the hut. She caught a glimpse of the interior, where two men were lying asleep on the floor. The cub, occasionally casting a side-glance at Margaret, proceeded to stir a thick yellow compound contained in a broken bowl. He then took a greasy spider and prepared to fry the not very appetizing batter into cakes. Here the father expostulated: "Hold up, Nathan; taint dinner-time yet by two hours. They uns can't eat a mess o' *your* fixin'."

The cub looked very shamefaced and, dropping his griddle, turned his back to Margaret and walked to the edge of the raft, where he stood with his hands in his pockets, whistling the air of a camp-meeting hymn. Margaret, who had seen his mortification, spoke to him as they were leaving the raft and thanked him for the trouble he had taken. The cub made no answer, but the back of his neck and his ears grew very red.

Miss Ruysdale had about her throat a crimson silk handkerchief, which she unfastened and laid in the old man's hand as he helped her to step on board the steamer. "Give this to Nathan from me," she whispered to him. As the little tug steamed briskly up the river, they saw the cub handling the square of silk very carefully. Then he brought out from his breeches pocket a piece of crumpled brown paper, and carefully wrapping Margaret's gift in it, he placed the packet in the leg of his boot for safety.

It was mid-day when they reached the plantation where Philip's childhood had 'been passed. As the steamer rounded the turn in the river which brought them in sight of the tall chimneys of the sugar-house, the whistle was sounded thrice. The signal was answered by a blast on an invisible horn, and by the time the boat was moored at the levee, a swarm of children of all sizes and colors had gathered upon the river-bank. Just as the gang-plank was thrown ashore, a carriage drove up at a smart pace, and a gentleman descended in time to assist the ladies to land.

Francis Rondelet, great-uncle to Philip, was a striking-looking old man, — tall and gaunt,

with a mass of thick white hair, fierce black
eyes and a kindly mouth which curiously belied
each other. He made his guests welcome with
a stately old-fashioned courtesy which impressed
Bouton de Rose immeasurably.

"He has the air of a duke," the young man
whispered to Mrs. Harden.

"Not at all," answered that imperturbable lady;
" he has the air of an American gentleman."

She loved a lord as dearly as most of us, but
she loved her birthright as a free and indepen-
dent American citizen still more, and would
allow no opportunity to pass in which she might
impress the young aristocrat with that fact. A
large carriage stood waiting for them ; and after
seeing his guests seated, the old man — he was
nearer to ninety than to eighty years — climbed
to the front seat and, taking the reins from the
boy who held them, guided the horses over the
rough and heavy road with a firm hand. The
old Rondelet house stood some way back from
the levee, the approach to it leading through
an avenue of mighty live-oaks. It was a pleasant habitation, built in the shape of a Maltese
cross, with wide galleries running around it and
a broad staircase leading from either side of the
entrance to the upper veranda. A wide hall
divided the whole length of the house, and from
it opened square, spacious rooms, cool and dim

with the twilight darkness of the Louisiana inte-
riors. The dining-room, separated from the hall
by an arched screen of exquisitely carved white
wood, was the first object of interest to the
hungry excursionists.

A dainty breakfast was served them by a pair
of pretty bronze handmaidens, whose beauty of
form and color delighted Margaret's artistic eye.
Mrs. Harden found the viands "utterly delicious," and complimented her host on the excellence of his coffee, his home-made wine, his
marvellous orange sweetmeats and. golden corn
bread. They sat together after the meal on the
shaded gallery until the sun was low in the horizon. General Ruysdale was much interested in
conversing with the old planter, whose mind was
wont to revert to the days when his plantation
produced three times as much cane as now, and
his fields teemed with the laborers who worked
without hire. General Ruysdale complimented
him on his fine estate and the healthy appearance of the negroes. The old man shook his
head and sighed.

"Ah, poor creatures," he said, "they are badly
off now — half clothed, badly fed. My dear sir,
it was a sad day for the negro when the responsibility of feeding and clothing himself was put
upon him. My men were dressed well, sir, —
two suits of clothes a year, of the best materials ;

good food, and all they could eat of it; doctors and medicines when they were sick; and regular work, sir. Not a spell of hard labor for two days, and then a debauch for three. Poor creatures! they are nothing but children, not fit to take care of themselves. I pity them myself; I do indeed. They were much better off before their so-called emancipation,—a thousand times better off."

"That may be so, Mr. Rondelet, I don't deny that there is a great deal of truth in what you say,"—Colonel Lagrange was the speaker,—"but *we* are a great deal better off without slavery. Emancipation of the blacks, General Ruysdale, you Northern folk talk so much about—it was n't the emancipation of an inferior African race that was of so much importance, it was the emancipation of the Southern whites, sir, from the curse of slavery, that made Abraham Lincoln a great man; and twenty years from now every intelligent man in the South, sir, will be of my opinion."

Francis Rondelet smiled incredulously at this speech. He could not accept these new opinions, so contradictory to the prejudices of the past. He waved his delicate white hand airily and said,—

"I cannot agree with you, Colonel. It must be the end of all order and public decency when men who have no sense of honesty are given an equal voice in the government with ourselves. The negroes all steal, sir. I never knew one that would n't steal. They have no idea of the sacredness of property."

"Is it not rather soon to expect people who have never owned any property, not even their own bodies, to develop a delicate sense of *meum* and *tuum?* How should they understand that which it has taken centuries of civilization to develop ever so little in ourselves? Give them property of their own, and that is the surest way to teach them to respect yours."

It was Margaret who spoke, blushing at her own temerity as soon as she had uttered the words.

"I think, Mademoiselle, that you have said the very best thing that could be said on the subject, which is in truth a vexed one," said Philip.

Margaret looked at him gratefully.

"What future seems to you to lie before the Southern negroes?" asked the General, addressing Colonel Lagrange.

"Can't say, sir. I should like to see them all shipped to Liberia. I believe that white men could do their work, and the country would be a deal better without them."

"There, sir, you are mistaken," interrupted the planter. "They are a necessity,—a necessary evil, I think we may call them ; and while Louisiana produces crops of sugar-cane, of rice, and of cotton, the negro must stay to gather them. To be sure, the measures which Congress seems about to adopt point to the direct crushing out of the sugar interests of the South. It is too lucrative a business for us to be permitted to carry on. Sugar brings seven cents a pound now, and when the duty is lifted, this estate, which to-day yields only half what it once did, will not pay for the planting. Strange times these ! "

The old man, spoke bitterly, and a moment's silence followed, broken at last by Bouton de Rose.

" I wish that I had seen La Louisiane in other times. It must have been very picturesque, slavery," he said, lightly.

" It is very picturesque now," said Margaret, " quite as full of romance and color as any life that I have ever seen in the old world."

Darius Harden, whose diplomatic soul had been tortured by the conversation, which could hardly fail to prove a heated one should it be allowed to go farther, seeing his opportunity to make a diversion, said : —

" I quite agree with you, Miss Margaret. It is cooler now ; will you not come and see the quarters ? "

" Willingly."

" And I also will go," said Bouton de Rose.
" I have no great knowledge of the affairs which
ces messieurs are discussing."

Mrs. Harden, who had been yawning behind
her fan, joined the party, and they took their
way to the negro-quarters, situated half a mile
from the house.

" What an enchanting little beast! What is
he ?" asked Margaret, stopping to admire a
bright-eyed, gray-furred creature tugging at the
end of its chain.

" That is Zillah, my uncle's pet coon. Is n't
she pretty ? Here, Coony, there 's something in
my pocket for you."

The coon sprang on Philip's shoulder, and its
curious little hands, delicate and horribly human,
fumbled in his pockets till they found a bit of
sugar. It cried plaintively when they left it, and
ran after them as far as its chain would permit.

Hero was their guide about the miniature
village. He introduced them to the preacher, a
young man of intelligent aspect, but who won
little favor among his parishioners, as Margaret
inferred from Hero's rather slighting comment:
" Bro' Peaseley 's a good man, but he is teruble
put to it for prayer ; he ain't got no gift of retri-
bution." Hero, who had been born and bred on
the plantation, was made very welcome by such

of the men and women as were not in the fields
at work. His old grandmother lived in a neat
whitewashed cabin shaded by a giant fig-tree.
She was of the pure African type, tall and
powerful, with a kindly old face threaded with a
web of wrinkles. Her head was bound up in a
bandanna handkerchief so arranged as to give
the effect of an impossibly elongated occipital
development. Her spotless white dress and
kerchief brought out her grotesque features as
a snood of ivory enhances the blackness of an
ebony mask. A dozen babies left in her care
rolled about on the clean sanded floor, yelping
and screaming like a litter of young puppies.
A broken pitcher, containing a bunch of yellow-
hearted lilies, stood on a shelf beside a young
mulatto woman who was sitting in the corner
suckling an infant. She was the embodiment of
physical beauty and strength, her color a warm
bronze, her features delicate and almost Greek in
their perfection of outline. The hands were
slim, and the bare feet high-instepped and aristocratic in shape. The strain of white blood
which had crossed the African in her must have
been a patrician one. She did not notice the
visitors, but went on crooning a low song to the
child in her arms. Hero ignored her presence
as completely as she failed to recognize his. He
spoke only to the old woman, never glancing at

the pretty figure with its short blue skirt and
low white bodice sitting so near him. The
grandmother, who was somewhat deaf, persisted in considering Margaret as a "missionary." She showed her her Bible and hymn-book,
holding the latter upside down in perfect un-
consciousness.

"What an Eve one could model from that girl
in her savage beauty!" said Margaret to Philip.
"She has a perfection of form and freshness of
face that seem to bring back the Woman of the
first Eden."

"And yet she is as finished an actress as the
most modern Eve. Would you have guessed
that that woman was the wife of my boy Hero,
and that she had not seen him until this moment for six weeks past? That is her idea of
etiquette."

"They are a curious people and very interesting," said Margaret. "I think it wonderful that
in little more than a century they should have
arrived at so high a degree of civilization as is
seen among the more educated ones to-day. In
the natural course of events, the social conditions
they now live in would not have been arrived at
in a thousand years and more."

"Margaret," said Mrs. Harden under her
breath, "you are talking about things of which
you are totally ignorant. They are hopelessly

immoral, these creatures, and there is no use in trying to teach them, how to behave themselves decently," she went on, speaking somewhat bitterly. " I hardly know a family to which some woman of that low race has not brought misery and shame. They are utterly depraved. You sympathize with *them;* I tell you it is their victims who deserve our pity."

" Is the fault altogether theirs that they have come to this pass ? " questioned Margaret. " How can people who for generations have had no idea of the sacredness of family life learn what it means in so few years ? Suppose your father had been sold into one State, your mother and sisters and brothers into another, — don't you think that you might have rather misty ideas about domestic relations ?."

" But that did n't happen outside of books, you know," answered Mrs. Harden. " Besides, they are perfectly untrustworthy — "

" And yet, Mrs. Harden, my uncle could, if he would, tell a very different story. During the war my father and himself and all the white men on the plantation were away from home fighting for the lost cause, and the women of the family were left here alone unprotected, at the mercy of these ' untrustworthy ' creatures, as you call them ; and what did they do ? Riot, steal, devastate, as white men would have done ? No, they protected the women, they worked the crops ; they were faithful, docile, obedient, as if the force which had once kept them so had not been broken forever. And this is not an isolated case, this was the rule all over the country ; and thus it was, by his self-restraint and forbearance, that the negro won the respect of the community, which no legal edict could ever have gained for him."

They had by this time reached the house ; and Francis Rondelet, who had caught his nephew's words, waved his white hand in gracious if somewhat condescending acquiescence.

" Yes, Philip, you are certainly right, their conduct was most praiseworthy. But what does it prove ? Simply that they were conscious of their inability to act and think for themselves. They went on automatically performing the tasks which they had been taught to accomplish. The negro is naturally a docile creature, quite docile."

He tapped the lid of his old silver snuff-box and took a pinch of maccaboy in a manner which seemed to dismiss the unwelcome topic of conversation.

He was a lonely old man, Francis Rondelet, his only companion in his quiet life an invalid niece, Philip's sister, who administered from her couch the affairs of the small household. The advent of his nephew's friends was a pleasant interruption to the monotony of existence on the plan-

tation, and it was late when they separated for
the night. Philip was in no mood for sleep. He
strolled down to the levee to smoke a cigar
and watch a certain window where a light still
burned. Across the white curtain a shadow
passed, vague yet graceful in its movements. He
stood with folded arms watching that small square
of light as intently as if a momentous issue hung
upon the reappearance of the shadow.

It passed again, this time more clearly defined.
He could trace the rounded outline of the bare
shoulders and the wavy sweep of unbound tresses
floating far below the waist. And then with a
burning blush he turned away, the feeling of a
shamed Acteon in his heart. He had been
too much absorbed to notice the approach of a
huge, shambling fellow, who came slouching up
to him and touched him on the shoulder.

" Marse Philip."

" Hero, is that you ? What are you doing
here at this time of night ? "

" It's a fine evening, Marse Philip."

Philip nodded silently, keeping his back reso-
lutely turned to the house.

" Never see the stars brighter," Hero continued.

He evidently had something to say, and Rondelet waited till he should gain time to shape his
thoughts.

" What sort of season does old Marse call it ? "

" Very good," answered Philip.

" Marse Philip."

A long pause followed. It was evident that Hero was summoning up his courage to speak his mind.

" Well, Hero."

" Marse Philip."

Another long pause, during which the ragged cap was removed and the left ear gently caressed.

" Marse Philip, why don't you git married ? "

" That's a hard question to answer, Hero. What makes you think that I want to marry ? "

" Marse Philip, you needs a wife to look arter you."

" A wife's an expensive luxury. You look after me very well. What would you have to do if I took a wife ? "

" A nigger can't take care of you, mor'n to brush you clothes and keep trashy folks from a cheating of you too much. 'T would be a real 'conomy for you to be married, Marse Philip ; wives is savin' folks."

" Indeed ! " Philip observed, remembering certain sums of money extorted from him by Hero under plea of matrimonial expenses.

" Thar's that young lady," Hero continued, " her with the yallar har. Why wouldn't she make you a good wife ? "

" Perhaps she would n't have me, Hero."

A low incredulous whistle was the only response to this remark:

" Besides, I can't afford to marry yet," Philip added. His pulses were beating at an absurd rate, and his face was bright with a light which was not reflected from the moon, a light of hope which shone through his deep gray eyes. The coarse-featured, clumsy creature beside him understood that look, and shifted his weight from one foot to the other uneasily.

" Marse Philip, you gwine to marry that young lady," he said at last, " and me and my wife 's a gwine to wait on yer. She 's good for wuk ; she 's lazed long enuff, I tell her. She 's smart, she is. We could keep you bof comfortable like; and 'bout the wages, why yer know, Marse Philip, yer 've paid me mor 'n I 'se worth for ten years, twice mor 'n, 'nd yer need n't think nothin' about *that*."

There was a moment's silence, and then Philip coughed very suddenly and relit his cigar.

" Thank you, Hero," he said when the spark was fairly kindled ; " thank you kindly, and good night."

The light had vanished from the corner window now, and with it the shadow of that lithe young figure, — a shadow which mixed itself wilfully all that night with Philip Rondelet's dreams.

CHAPTER XIII.

THE garden is the fairest spot in all the wide Rondelet plantation. Here the lilies are all ablow, lining the paths in stately rows and nodding gravely at one another as Margaret walks between them, brushing the dew from their petals with the sweep of her white robe. She passes under an amethyst canopy of wistarias ; and leaning against the old tree about which the vine has flung its freshness, she pauses and breathes in the beauty of the scene. A thick hedge of Cherokee-roses screens the garden from the house and offices. Here is no hint of work or business ; it is a place to dream in, a place to love in, a place to lie in at peace, when life and love and work are over. Dark and straight, a pair of aged cypresses rise from the midst of all the bloom and perfume of countless flowers. Between the two quiet sentinels is a tomb, lichen-stained, grass-grown. The letters are now untraceable. The Great Mother has blurred out the words which tell by what name, at what time, her child lived and moved above the breast wherein he now lies. Soft-furred, silvery moss gently veils these details, unimportant now; but one word of all the inscription is spared, — "Peace." Margaret, pausing by this sepulchre, breathes a deep sigh; and leaning upon the sculptured urn, reads the lesson of mortality, so often learned, so oft forgotten.

Far off, at the opposite corner of the garden, stands a pavilion, whose sides and roof seem woven of living jasmine and honeysuckle. Here breakfast has been prepared, and hither Sara Harden comes, dainty and fresh as a shepherdess of romance. Her fair, curling hair is gathered high on her head beneath a distracting little hat, all blue ribbons and roses. Her skin is admirably set off by the pale blue of her Watteau dress, and her dewy infantine eyes shine like deep forget-me-nots. A perfectly pretty woman is Sara Harden; beautiful, no one who knows the value of that superlative term would call her. There are no grand lines, no mysterious coming and going of light and shadow in her delicate face; no moments of loveliness obscured for a time and then shining out radiant and all powerful; nothing of the half-painful influence which great beauty holds for those who are enamored of it, — nothing of this has the bonny shepherdess, only a restful, pleasure-giving prettiness, which makes men grateful and even women glad, as they are glad of a beautiful child or a perfect flower.

From the steps of the little pavilion Sara Harden, standing in a flood of sunlight, perceives Margaret's white drapery beneath the sombre cypress.

"Margaret! Margaret—O Mar-ga-ret!"

A handkerchief is waved in answered greeting from the shadowy corner of the garden.

"Come here, I say; don't you hear me?" She had not said it before.

Stopping only to gather a shaft of golden lilies, Margaret comes obedient to the small tyrant of the iron will and caressing voice.

"Where have you been? How white you look—b-r-r-r-r-r! what were you doing in the one dark spot of all this pleasant garden? An unhealthy creature, mousing about in creepy corners instead of sunning yourself in the summer-house."

Margaret has drawn near by this time, and stands, with a sad smile on her face, looking at the joyous creature before her, thoughtlessly happy, full of health and brilliant vitality.

"You have been prowling about that old, forgotten tomb with an uncanny joy that is positively immoral. What do you mean by wearing that look of stoical gloom, in the face of this glorious morning, in the anticipation of a good breakfast ? Ingrate, look at me."

"You would make the most confirmed stoic smile, you are so delightfully gay," said Margaret, with a little sigh.

" My dear, *you* are now in the gloom of youth ; I have passed through it myself. I, even I, — the frivolous, the light-headed, — have felt much of the sort of sorrow which is now vexing you. It is, in a way, an imaginary sorrow. You are learning the realities of life ; you are finding out that Death and Grief and Love and Sin are not purely allegorical figures sculptured on the walls which bound your life-path, but real creatures, with which you must grapple and wrestle, which you must conquer or be conquered by, not once, but a thousand times. You are finding this out. You have read of these four personages, you have seen many pictures of them, you have perhaps typified them with your own hands ; but you have never realized their existence till now."

Margaret shook her head and straightened a fold of her friend's gown. She had a profound conviction that the feelings to which she was now a prey had never been experienced before, and that her debonair friend was incapable of suffering as she suffered ; and yet Sara Harden bore a wound in her heart which not even time had healed, — the grief of a mother

for her only child, the pity of a wife for her
childless husband. She smiled and touched
Margaret's pale cheek with her rosy lips, — a
woman who had loved and suffered, and was
strong to bear the burden of her grief so that
its shadow might not darken the life of any
other human creature.

To these two fair women came Philip Rondelet, the old planter leaning on his arm, Colonel
Lagrange, General Ruysdale, Bouton de Rose,
and Darius Harden following. Soon after was
served a breakfast of honey, whose sweetness
had been gathered from the flowers of the garden, of butter and cream, for which a pair of
black-nosed Jerseys cropping the grass near by
were responsible, of fish caught in the neighboring bayou, eggs from the farm-yard, bread light
and sweet as the most fastidious sybarite could
desire, and coffee, that Creole coffee, of unsur-
passed fragrance and flavor. They lingered
over the table, for it was the last meal they
were to take together, and host and guests were
equally sorry that the brief visit had come to
an end.

The quiet of the morning was suddenly broken
by the faint echo of a whistle. "Alack! it is
the steamer," cried Mrs. Harden ; "that means
that we must leave this enchanting place, perhaps
forever."

Twenty minutes later they were standing on the river-bank watching the approach of the mammoth white boat. Handkerchiefs were waved, and in answer to this primitive signal the huge craft, cleverly handled as an Indian's canoe, drew along-side the levee. The gangway was thrown, and while the monster held its breath for a moment, the friends were safely transferred to the lower deck; another sixty seconds, and the steamer was on her course again, the group of new passengers in her stern waving a last greeting to the spare old man standing hat in hand beneath a giant live-oak gray and venerable as himself.

The steamer had a fair number of passengers, and was heavily freighted with cotton. Groups of men smoking, talking, and playing cards were collected on her decks and in the after-saloon.

Most of them were rough-looking fellows enough, drovers from Texas, horse-traders from everywhere, rancheros from the Far West, and a gang of Chinamen bound for South America to labor in a climate too deadly even for the negro. Railroads must be built, rivers must be spanned, mountains must be tunnelled for the march of commerce; and for these things, which the American covets but cannot achieve, the despised Mongolian is imported, and treated as the African never was, execrated and scoffed at by a nation which owes no little of its prosperity to-day to his tireless, uncomplaining industry.'

Captain Silas Martin, a burly fellow born beside the river and bred to thread its ever-shifting channels, was an old acquaintance of Colonel Lagrange. He made that worthy man and his friends heartily welcome to the good ship " Crescent Queen," of which he was part owner and sole commander. He was a jovial soul, full of native wit and abounding in anecdotes of his life upon the river. He remembered one trip made in the old troublous times, when he had stood at the wheel under the guard of two armed Union officers who watched him day and night. One false turn of the wheel in that puzzling, sinuous channel, and his life would have been forfeit.

He had been captured, and placed at the wheel of a war transport bound from New Orleans to a point higher up the river with a cargo of ammunition and stores. Of little use were the government pilots, — Northern men, — on a river which from week to week shifts its course, now swerving to the right and stealing a piece of territory on that side, and leaving a shoal on the other hand, again building an island or washing away a spit of the soft bottom land. One who belonged to the freemasonry of Mississippi pilots must guide the

boat, and Silas Martin was chosen as the like-
liest man to bring the precious freight to its
destination. He had brought the transport
safely up the river ; he loved his life, and he
loved his own word. Both were pledged to the
young officers, who never left him, sleeping or
waking.

"Is not the 'Crescent Queen' a very fast
boat, Captain Martin ?" asked Margaret.

"She is called so, miss. Colonel Lagrange
there can tell you something of her speed."

But the Colonel only nodded an assent to this
remark, and a few moments after drew Margaret to the other side of the deck, from which
was to be had a view of a late crevasse. Half a
hundred men were at work on the levee fighting
the river which had brought desolation to the
plantation and ruin to the crops. The lawn was
still submerged, and the blossoms of the taller
rose-bushes looked over the invading water,
blighted, but not yet dead. A row-boat was
moored outside the door of the manor-house,
whose broad stone steps were half covered by
the tide.

"What havoc the river has made here !" said
Margaret. "But it was not only to see this that
you brought me away from the others ?"

"No, my dear young lady ; you had opened a
dangerous topic of conversation. The last time

I heard Captain Martin questioned about the speed of the 'Crescent Queen' the consequences were rather serious.   There was a new boat on the river.   The Captain was afraid of her, I think ; but when she blew the signal for a race, he ordered our speed increased.   All the passengers begged Martin not to accept the challenge, but he answered them pretty roughly. The new boat pressed us hard, and I saw our furnace crammed with barrels of oil, with crates of fruit, with cotton and freight.   No matter what, anything that would burn was tossed into the roaring fire ; but the new boat gained on us.   I had bet all the money in my pockets on the 'Crescent Queen.'   There was not a man on board, down to the nigger firemen, who had not put up something on the race.   I remember I asked the Captain if he thought we should beat her.   He was at the speaking-tube, and roared out, 'Send up my whiskey — straight ;' then turning to me he said, 'Beat her, sir, or bust!' It did not quite come to that, for by the time we had reached a narrow turn in the river the rival boat had almost caught up with us ; there was not room for both steamers abreast, and in a flash Martin turned the 'Queen's' head and drove her bow straight into the side of the other boat.   She never raced again, I believe, and the 'Crescent Queen' has not been challenged since.

That was some years ago. Things are changed
now, and the times are quieter," the Colonel
added, with a sigh which Margaret interpreted,
perhaps unjustly, as an expression of regret at
the altered conditions of travel on the Mississippi.

Margaret's stateroom commanded a view of
the deck ; and when, late that evening, she
opened her door and prepared to steal out for
a last look at the river, she found herself confronted by a group of card-players. One of
them might have been, judging from his dress,
a clergyman. The other two were rough-looking
fellows, one of whom was greatly excited. He
smote the table with his clenched hand, mut-
tering fierce imprecations. Visions of Mr. Jack
Oakhurst crossed Margaret's mind ; that deli-
cate-featured young man, with the correct broadcloth suit and melancholy blue eyes, must belong
to the same class as that gambler hero, and the
red-faced drover and his friend were probably
being " plucked." So great was the young girl's
interest in the card-players that she had failed
to notice three men who had come on board at
the last stop ; not so Philip Rondelet, whom
people were wont to call unobservant. He had
seen the pair of man-hunters push their manacled
prisoner upon the lower deck and chain him by
a ring in the gunwale to a log of wood, whereon

he sat, or rather crouched. The prisoner was a negro of the most degraded type ; a criminal, one could not doubt him to be. Crime was stamped upon his low, animal forehead and frightful wolfish features with terrible distinctness. So much the occupants of the saloon-deck noted at a glance ; and seeing that, thought no more of the writhing creature swaying on his rough seat with every motion of the boat. But Philip Rondelet, to whom it was given to see all of pain and suffering that crossed his path, observed that the prisoner was suffering keenly. He passed Margaret's half-open door without a glance, went down the companion-way, and addressed one of the men in charge of the prisoner : " That man seems to be in great pain."

" Think likely," was the laconic reply. The captive groaned. Philip saw that his arm was wounded and in need of care.

" I am a surgeon," he continued, " and I mean to dress that wound."

" Hands off my prisoner, young man. I don't stand no interference in my affairs," brutally protested the guardian of the law.

" Excuse me, sir," — Philip's voice was as courteous and sweet as if he had been addressing Margaret herself, — " but I consider this to be *my* affair ; and it is I who will brook no interference."

He moved nearer the prisoner. The officer with an oath started to his feet; and laying his hand on Philip's shoulder, warned him as he loved his life not to lay a finger on the negro.

The dispute had attracted the attention of some of the passengers, though the card-players had not looked up from their game. The instant the officer touched Rondelet, the physician wrenched himself from his grasp, and placing himself beside the negro, said in a voice whose silver tones, though hardened to steel, had lost nothing of their polish: "I am a doctor of medicine. This man is badly hurt, and I propose to dress his wound. I am alone and unarmed, but I mean to put this thing through."

His voice never shook, though he was covered by the revolver in the bully's hand.

There was a stir among the passengers.

"I'll play you double or quits on the next game," said the red-faced drover. "And now, young man, go ahead with your splintering, and I'll stand by to see fair play, if it's only to stop that nigger's d— noise."

He shuffled the cards, handed them to the clerical-looking young man, and cocking his seven-shooter, pointed it at the officer. Quick to see the altered situation, the latter lowered his weapon. It was evident that public sym-

pathy was with the physician, who was already
at work tearing his fine linen handkerchief into
narrow strips to form a bandage. The clerical
gentleman fetched some water in a tin cup; and
then, resuming his seat, dealt the cards, and the
game was taken up at the point where it had
been interrupted. Rondelet sponged the ugly
wound and deftly disposed the linen· bandage
about the arm.

"Now loosen those handcuffs," he said authoritatively.

"I 'll see you damned first," growled the
officer.

"Unlock those bracelets, — do you hear? —
before I count three.   The game's mine."

It was the drover who spoke, fingering his
revolver as he did so.

The fetters were taken from the prisoner's
wrists.

"Undo the chain that holds him to the log,"
said Philip.

The officer swore under his breath; but after
a glance at the faces of the men about him,
complied.

Philip made his patient as comfortable as he
could under the circumstances, and after giving
him an opiate, turned and left the lower deck.

Margaret had witnessed the whole scene.
She did not speak to him as he passed her

door on his way to the forward deck, where
Mrs. Harden was sitting.

"What has happened to you, Philip?" Sara
Harden asked as soon as he joined her. He
told her what had passed.

She looked at him admiringly, and laid a soft,
gemmed hand on his arm.

" Philip, you are a person for an emergency.
How excited you look! See, your hand is positively trembling."

" Yes? as long as it was firm while I probed
the wound, what does it matter ?" He was nettled by what she had said.

" Philip, I don't believe in platonics, and yet
I positively love you at this moment, — do you
know what I mean ? — without being a particle
in love with you."

" What is the distinction ? "

" When one loves a person, it is a disinterested
feeling ; when one is in love, one wants the person for one's own. Now I certainly am not in
love with you, for I should n't know what to do
with you if you were given to me this moment ;
and yet I am quite certain that I love you as I
might love a child, — and yet you are a great
deal better and stronger than I am — "

" You are very good to me, dear friend."

" I wish I could be really good to you, but I
cannot ; you are so quaint and misty and intan-

gible, I am never quite sure about you. But there, of course you don't care what I feel about you; the blind of Miss Ruysdale's stateroom is infinitely more interesting to you than anything I can say."

Philip looked penitent, and made an effort to keep his eyes from wandering in the direction of Margaret's room.

" You really love her so much ? "

" You know," he answered simply.

" Yes, and I know she is n't worthy of it." She was irritated, and spoke sharply.

" It hurts me to hear you say that, dear friend," he protested.

" She 's a good, sweet, honest girl," Mrs. Harden continued, " but she no more appreciates you, nor the worth of what you give her, than a royal baby knows the value of his jewelled coral. He breaks it just as carelessly as another child smashes a twopenny rattle. Margaret plays with your heart just as if it were not a solid lump of refined gold, but a miserable pinchbeck thing, like most men's hearts, to be gilded and regilded any number of times to suit the requirements of each new passion."

" If it is hers to do as she likes with ? "

" But she will neither take it nor leave it. I know just what she will do, — she will trifle with it till — "

" Listen to me," interrupted Philip. " You say my heart is purer than some other men's. I know not whether this is so ; but if it be true, it is because she has purified it, it is because of my love for her. That is my treasure. Whether I win her love or not, I have always my love for her. You pity me, — *me*, who would rather a thousand times give up life itself than outgrow my love. Happy or unhappy, it is more to me than all else. Could I believe for a moment that I could survive this love, I should pray that I might die to-night."

" It is not often that we women are loved like that, Philip," said Sara Harden very gravely. " I believe I shall think better of men all my life for what you have said to me to-night. You have lifted your whole sex in my estimation, *mon ami ;* and this is not the first noble lesson that you have taught me, nor will it be the last. It is something for a man to feel that he is understood and appreciated even by a woman with whom he is not in love. Believe me, I know the value of your true heart and your honest hand. And now I must go inside. Good night to you ; Dari is waiting for me."

CHAPTER XIV.

ON the day when our party of friends had left the city, Robert Feuardent also went into the country. The magnet which had kept him in New Orleans for so many weeks was now removed, and he took the opportunity to visit his forest-home. Many months had elapsed since he had shaken the dust of the city from his feet, and despite the heavy feeling at his heart, his spirits began to rise as he left the noise and tumult of the streets behind him. His emotions that morning had been far from enjoyable as he watched the departure of his friends for the Rondelet plantation. He had concealed himself behind a pile of cotton-bales standing conveniently near that part of the levee from which they had embarked, and had marked that they all seemed in very good spirits. Every mile that he put between himself and the scene of that annoyance seemed to lighten the jealous anger that had galled him.

What felon in his chains, what sufferer from a grievous disease, what mourner for a beloved one dead, is to be more pitied than that man or woman in whose soul jealousy has taken up its abode? It is, I believe, the most grievous passion that can séar the heart of man. What crimes will he not commit to appease that demon in his breast, whose presence banishes every tender and human sentiment? If he be driven by jealousy to the commission of the unpardonable sin, if he shed the life-blood of brother or of wife, what council of his peers but will judge that the demon was stronger than his humanity, and that, just or unjust, his crime must be condoned?

It was on the very edge of night that Robert arrived at the little settlement of friendly Indians. He found the wigwams deserted by all save the women and old men. After resting for a few moments, he proceeded to the chapel of the missionary priest, situated at a short distance from the hamlet. His way led him over a dilapidated bridge which spanned a bayou contiguous to the great lake. He stepped lightly over the loose-lying planks, which would have failed to support any less wary wayfarer. He knew just how to throw his weight, and could spring from a rotten board before it gave way beneath him. He was midway on his somewhat perilous journey when he was hailed by a cheerful voice; a wagon was fording the bayou, and he recognized in its driver an old acquaintance. The horses stopped, obedient to their master's "Whoa, Emma! whoa, Baby!" and stood patiently still in the water, which reached up to the hubs of the wheels.

"Won't you come up to the house and dine with us? I have a seat for you in the carriage," asked the driver. He had a cheery voice and kind blue eyes, and the group of children, of all sizes and ages, packed about him echoed the invitation in chorus.

"Do come up, Robert, and see my new pony," cried a boy, evidently the eldest.

"Monsieur Feuardent, you never made the kite you promised me," said a demure little girl.

"We've got some new puppies," vouchsafed a' chubby urchin of four.

"We're going to have a great big turkey for dinner," added a wise maiden of six, who at an early age had divined the surest road to the masculine heart.

Which argument was the convincing one, I cannot say. Perhaps it was the combined attractions of the "great big turkey" and the "puppies," or it may have been that the prospect of seeing the new pony was too enticing to be resisted; in any case the fact is certain that five minutes later Robert was seated in the carriage beside M. Bienveillance, with a child on either knee.

"I was on my way to seek the Father," explained Robert.

"I am in luck to have met you, then, for he dines with us to-night."

"And there's going to be *such* a big jelly-cake," whispered the little six-year-old.

"He is well? it is many months since I have seen him," said Feuardent.

"Yes, well as ever," replied M. Bienveillance; "though how he endures such discomforts at his age, amazes me. A wonderful man, sir, and the best human being I have ever known. My wife says his sainthood has begun on this side of eternity."

By this time the sure-footed horses had struggled up the incline which led to the bayou, and the carriage was on firm ground again. The road before them led through a thick swampy country, rich with the luxuriance of an almost tropical vegetation. The broad shining leaves of the palmetto overshadowed a thousand smaller plants not less beautiful than itself. In a cleared space, where the ground was high, a group of cattle ceased munching the herbage and turned their great eyes wonderingly at the carriage as it rolled by. A flock of sheep, whose long fleecy wool had left traces on the low underbrush, were browsing under the care of a dusky shepherd who saluted the master as he passed. 'The carriage stopped before a cottage whose wide-roofed piazza was wreathed with honeysuckle. A lady, sitting in a low chair, rose to meet Feuardent, and bade him welcome to her forest-home. She smiled at her husband as she gave her hand to her guest, and said in a sweet, gracious voice, "You are never more welcome, *mon cher* than when you bring with you so agreeable a guest as M. Feuardent."

The conversation was carried on entirely in French. Madame Bienveillance was a tall, handsome woman with large dark eyes and a red, curved mouth. Her complexion was white and flawless as the thick creamy leaves of the magnolia blossom which drooped from the ribbon at her waist. Her smile seemed to Feuardent as innocent as that which rested on the features of the child clinging to her skirts. She did the honors of her simple home with a gracious hospitality often found wanting in more pretentious houses. Her summer-dwelling possessed only four rooms, gathered about a large chimney. These were her own apartment, a guest-chamber, a parlor, and a dining-room rarely used in weather which allowed the table to be spread on the gallery. Near by, another cottage of similar dimensions afforded sleeping and play-rooms to the children;

a third building was reserved for such guests as were happy enough to enjoy the hospitality of the amiable couple.

" What news do you bring us from the city? M. Feuardent, I shall consider you in the light of an animated society-newspaper, through whose columns I may gather something of what my friends in New Orleans are doing," said Madame Bienveillance.

Poor Robert was at a loss to answer her. He had lived so entirely in his own emotions for weeks past that he had neither thought nor cared about the rest of the world. He only knew about Margaret ; and he was on the point of yielding to the lover's impulse to talk of his beloved, even to a stranger, when a step was heard on the path and a tall, gaunt figure approached them.

" *Mon père*, you are most welcome ; it is long since you have broken bread with us," the lady said, greeting the new-comer affectionately.

" It is not longer ago than this morning since I have eaten of thy bread, my daughter. My other friends say that thou dost more than thy share in keeping my larder supplied. How is this, — Robert Feuardent, the deserter, here ? Thy wigwam has lost its roof, thy friends have almost forgotten thy face, thy dogs acknowledge a new master. What hast thou found in the

15

city so attractive that thou hast so neglected those whom thou hast professed to love above all others ? "

Robert hung his head and blushed like a school-boy detected in some naughty prank.

The keen-eyed old man looked at him closely for a moment, and seeing his perturbation, turned to the children, who had come to speak with him. The priest was a remarkable-looking man, who carried his threescore and ten years lightly. His face was a variable one. When it was bent, as now, over the little children, it was tender and full of light ; so it looked when he walked among his Indians, to whose welfare he had devoted the greater part of his life. They had adopted him as a member of their tribe, and the name they had given him signified the affection in which they held him. His broad philanthropic brow, his large, kindly mouth, betrayed the lover of men, satisfied in giving up his life for their advancement ; but the quick, restless dark eyes sometimes had a look of profound sorrow in their depths, of whose source Robert had often vainly conjectured. Madame Bienveillance, with her quicker womanly instinct, saw in this trait of melancholy, whose existence the priest would have eagerly denied, the result of some great trial or disappointment suffered during his life in that world which he now apostro-

phized as heartless, godless, loveless. For him
the solitude of the woods, the companionship of
the wild men, the song of the forest bird, sufficed.
He wondered that men of heart and intellect
could endure the stifling atmosphere of cities,
and claimed that only through that intimacy
with Nature which the solitudes of the wilder-
ness afford can the soul rise to the height of
communion with the Divine. Yet toward that
world which he had quitted, and of which he
spoke such hard things, his thoughts ever turned,
if it was but to compare it with the paradise he
claimed to have found in the deserted places.

The evening passed quickly and pleasantly.
Robert's melancholy was soon dispelled by the
cheerful influences of the happy home circle.
Shortly after dinner he disappeared in company
with the children, the two younger ones seated
on his broad shoulders and clinging about his
neck with the remorseless grip of a pair of
young grislies.

"Do not stifle your kind friend," cautioned
Madame Bienveillance. But the youngsters only
screamed louder than before, and the smaller
boy on the left shoulder buried his hands in
Robert's hair, crying, —

"When one rides without bridle, one must
hold on by the mane."

"When one rides without spurs, one must

use one's heels," echoed the child on the right shoulder, suiting the action to the word.

In a moment the obstreperous rider was landed on a high shelf, from which he was only lifted on parole of good behavior. The puppies were next visited and duly admired. They were the property of the little six-year-old girl.

"Monsieur Feuardent shall have one of the · puppies," she cried. "Choose whichever one you want, you can have any of them except the white one, because I named him for papa,— he is so fat; and the spotted one, I gave that one to my big brother; and this one, which is a little lame, I must keep him myself, because no one else will be so kind to him."

"That only leaves Robert the ugly little black fellow. Papa says he is not worth raising; that is the reason you are so generous with him,— Greedy," teased the big brother.

The child began to cry, and presently sobbed out, —

"I am sure I am not greedy, and it is very mean of you to say so. I gave you your first choice, but you shall not have him now. I always liked the spotted one best myself."

"You did n't; you don't know enough," retorted the boy. "It is only because I said he was the best marked, and you only *pretended* to give me my choice, so as to find out which

was the best one, and then take it back from me
the first chance you got, — just like girls ! "

" I like the black one best," interposed Robert.
" Black dogs are better for grown people than
white, or even spotted ones."

The little girl smiled through her tears and
laid the ugly black creature in Robert's hand.
The boy looked somewhat sceptical, but he did
not quite dare to question Mr. Feuardent's last
statement ; and the puppy being carefully laid in
a small basket packed with straw, a game of
romps ensued, which rivalled the antics of the
most playful of puppies. Bedtime came all too
soon, and the playfellows parted regretfully,
Robert joining the elders at the main house,
carrying his basket on his arm. The gifts of
children are very serious matters to them, and
Robert was too tender-hearted to refuse the ugly
little creature yelping in its straw nest.

He found the missionary in an excellent vein.
He was recounting to Madame Bienveillance
some of the incidents of the forty years passed
among the Louisiana Indians, and Robert, seating himself, listened to the stories, some of which
were already known to him. He had been for
years so familiar with the life of this solitary old
man that he had perhaps sometimes ignored its
beauty and its pathos. The outlines of things
at which we look too closely are sometimes

blurred; those who stand at a distance often get the true values which we miss by being too near. Robert was very silent as they drove afterward to the home of the priest, where he was to pass the night. M. Bienveillance, who had accompanied them so far, took leave of Robert, cordially inviting him to return to his house the following day. The kindly man, whose name so well expressed his nature, touched his horses with the whip, and was soon lost to view as the carriage disappeared down the narrow wood-road. They heard his cheery voice calling to his animals in the distance, and then the silence of the forest settled down upon them.

The home of the priest was situated under a spreading live-oak whose undermost branches scarcely cleared the roof of the lowly structure. The rough wooden building, had it not been dignified by the cross which rose above it, canopied by the spreading branches of the tree, might have passed for the cabin of a wood-cutter. Its interior was hardly superior to the outside. A few rough benches, some religious pictures on the wall, and an altar as simple as was the priest who officiated before it, — these were all it contained. At one end a small space was partitioned off from the church, and here was spread the couch of the missionary, — a blanket thrown over a bed of bare wooden planks.

"Thou knewest how thou wouldst fare with me, Robert, when thou didst decline to remain with our friends," said the priest.

"I have not yet forgotten how to cut my bed from the pine-branches, father, though it is long since I have slept on such a fragrant mattress," Robert returned.

"And why hast thou remained so many months away from thy friends? Thou lovest not the confessional, I know, but speak to me as to thy friend. Thou hast a burden on thy heart, Robert; thou art not the free, light-hearted youth thou wert a year ago."

The young man hesitated, loath to grieve his friend with the recital of the troublous events of the past winter. The priest was so far removed from the world's grossness that it seemed a wrong to desecrate his forest-chapel with a story of passion, of bloodshed, of cowardice, of deceit, and of human love.

"Speak, my son," said the priest authoritatively.

The old habit of obedience prevailed, and Robert complied with the father's exhortation to confide in him.

The hour was late when the two friends lay down to sleep, the priest on his hard bed, the youth on the floor beside him. The silence of the woods, the fatigues he had endured, and the

freshness of his fragrant couch insured a long
sleep to Feuardent. The sun was high in the
heavens when he awoke. He found beside him
a pitcher of water, bread and meat, and a cup
of coffee, fragant and inviting, prepared by the
father's own hands. It was Sunday morning,
and from the sounds in the adjoining chapel
Robert judged that preparations for service were
in progress. Dressing noiselessly, he made his
escape through the window and betook himself
to the Indian settlement, not far distant. While
the priest was ministering to the spiritual needs
of his dusky flock, Robert, in company with a
pair of Sabbath-breaking redskins, went on a
hunting tour, the result of which was highly
favorable to the larder of his host. Through
the well-known haunts he tramped, whistling as
he went an old Creole love-song, his gun on his
shoulder, his dogs following him. He was thinking joyfully of Margaret ; yesterday's dark mood
had been dispelled by the scenes and faces which
were so familiarly dear to him, and by the counsels of that wise old man who had so little of
this world about him.

Robert Feuardent felt all the beauty of his
forest home because something in him claimed
kindred with the wood-life. He felt but could
not express the delights of an existence governed
only by the laws of Nature. The priest, who

was born a poet, was never weary of contrasting
the peace of the forest with the turmoil of the
world in which he had suffered so keenly, and
which he could never quite forget. The glowing panegyrics which he pronounced upon the
desert which had so hospitably sheltered him
had been listened to by Robert in other days
with scant attention. The world, which the
priest had characterized as " barbarously sophis-
tical " and "coldly refined," had been to him a
pleasant place enough. He had found friends
and amusements there, and had lived its life as
thoughtlessly and gayly as he had lived the forest
life. He had on the whole preferred the companionship of the wood people ; but not because
he found the world people heartless or cruel. It
had been a mere matter of taste with him. *Now,*
he saw things very differently. He listened to
the words of the missionary with an unwonted
attention ; he realized how the pure-minded man
must have been outraged by the shams and
the lies, the selfishness and cruelty, of society.
"The rottenness of the great world" had, to
use his own words, "forced him to fly from it,
as from a pestilential corpse, to the forest which
God made as a refuge for man when every other
refuge is denied him."

By sundown Robert had come back from his
day's hunting, and the two men were sitting before

the door of the little chapel, under the shade of the friendly oak. A half-caste Indian boy was seated near them, busily engaged in stripping the birds Robert had shot. The huntsman himself was cleaning his gun ; his dogs lay at his feet. The black puppy, which had already made friends with them, was rolling over the tired creatures, who were too sleepy to heed the impudent youngster.

"What you say may be true, father," said Robert, gathering a wisp of grass which he rammed vigorously into, the barrel of his fowling-piece ; " but look at the woods. Things die and decompose here ; but new flowers bloom every day from what yesterday was foul decay. Look now at this piece of wood," — he paused in his work and picked up a branch, — " it is quite rotten, it has lain in the water for months ; but to-day this beautiful pink flower has bloomed from it. Is not this same thing going on in the world ? "

The priest did not answer directly. He looked at his young friend silently for a few moments, and then said : "Dost thou think that thou canst understand the world ? Thou art but a boy."

" I have grown ten years older in the last six months," persisted the younger man ; " I am a boy no longer ; and I now know that I can never live as you do, away from the world."

" I have never counselled it, Robert."

" No, father, you have not. You have said to
me that I must try to live with civilized men,
and that not till I had seen, as you have seen,
their falseness and their barbarity, could I enjoy
deliverance from their society. I once listened
to you, and I believed you. Now I know that I
am not strong enough to live alone as you have
done. I need the contact with other men, even
if they are sinful. I am sinful too ; and as I
am sorry for them, so will they be for me. As
I am glad when they are happy, so will they
rejoice with me."

" Alone, saidst thou, alone ? " cried the enthu-
siast, ignoring the rest of the sentence, " O
sightless eyes that cannot see ! O deaf ears that
cannot hear ! I have the immaculate maiden
Nature for my companion. What woman wilt
thou show me with such infinite variety of loveliness ? Each day her face wears a new expression ; every hour her mood changes ; whether
she smile or frown, she is always faithful, always
tender. If she whispers to me in the soft mur-
murings of the night, if she sings to me with
the voice of the wood-bird, if she soothes me
with the wind sighing through the trees, if her
voice startles me in the crash of the thunder
and calls me in the mighty melody of the river,
it is to tell me with each of her myriad voices
that she loves me."

The priest had risen, speaking passionately, his hands clasped, his eyes raised to the towering oak-tree, through whose branches the sunbeams filtered about him like a glory. Robert, still busy with his gun, glanced at the inspired face, and with a sigh went on with his work.

"Madame Bienveillance is right," he said to himself; "he is a saint already."

Meanwhile the boy had finished his task; and after building a fire in the hollow stump of a tree, proceeded to broil the game after the approved Indian fashion. When it was ready, he laid the table, — a service which was speedily accomplished, for the best of reasons. When the simple preparations were complete, the child, whose reverence for the inspired moods of the priest was not equal to Robert's, who would never have dared to call that pure spirit from its lofty communings, pulled the missionary by the arm and pointed silently to the table.

"Robert, I have not fared so well since thou wert last here. Tell me, does the New Orleans market afford such trout as these, such a pair of ducks?"

"Yes, father, I think it does," answered Robert, eying the smoking viands hungrily; "it is the appetite that is lacking in the city."

He moved toward the table.

"See the delicate markings on this fish!"

continued the priest; "I wonder thou hadst the heart to keep him for thy prey, he is so beautiful a creature."

Robert's nostrils were tickled by the crisp fragrance of the roasted trout.

"I am too busy in smelling the fish, and shall soon be in tasting it, I hope, to care much for its markings," cried Robert. "*Don't* let the good food get cold, father."

"Thou art hungry indeed, Robert," answered the priest; and making no further delay, he asked the blessing, without which Robert would not have dared to touch a crust of his bread. The two friends sat down side by side on a rough bench, and the dusky child served them silently.

"We do not often feast like this, do we, my boy?" said the priest kindly.

The child shook his head, still speechless.

"Whose son is this?" asked Robert; "he must be a stranger, since he will not speak before me."

"Yes; thou hast never seen him before," returned the missionary. "The fact that my Indians refuse to enter into conversation with strange white people is not without a sad significance," he added; "they have been so abused by the dominant — I cannot call it the superior — race, that they suspect all of its children who fall in their way. This boy here knows, young

as he is, that he may say too much if he talks
before you. You are, in his eyes, probably a
government agent, and he has been taught that
they are to be distrusted, even when they make
friendly overtures. They fear the Greeks bringing gifts."

" Why, what have the Greeks got to do with
the Indians or the government ?" queried Robert, filling and lighting his pipe as he spoke.

" Thou didst not love thy studies at school, or
thou wouldst not ask. Of the knowledge that is
had from books, Robert, thou art sadly ignorant ;
and in this thou art wrong. There is yet time
for thee to cultivate a love of learning ; thy mind
is good. Like the Indians, thou never forgettest
what thou hast seen or heard. I, too, have a
keen memory ; and how richly is it peopled with
the heroes of the poets ! When thou art old
like me, and canst no more spend thy leisure
in hunting and breaking wild horses, how wilt
thou pass thy time ? Do as I have done, and
take from men their noblest inspirations. My
solitude has for its companions the men and
women born in the dreams of the great writers
of the world. In leaving that world behind
me, I took with me the best things that it has
produced."

The father's speech was here interrupted by
an Indian woman, who rushed from the thicket,

and throwing herself at his feet besought him
to come to her husband, who was either dying
or bewitched. The good man stopped only to
gather together those necessaries of spiritual
and physical ministration which the sufferer
might require, — a few phials of medicine and
the vessels for the sacrament of extreme unc-
tion, — and disappeared down the woodland
path, followed by the weeping woman. The boy
having fed himself, the dogs, and the puppy,
quenched the embers of the fire with water
from the spring near by, and nodding to Robert,
departed without a word of greeting, taking the
same direction as the priest.

With only his dogs for company, Robert sat
before the chapel, watching the death of the day,
and the night darkening in the skies and through
the odorous forest. He listened to those silent
noises of the night which are felt rather than
heard, and in his mind reviewed all the things
the priest had said to him. He had been in the
forest only twenty-four hours, and yet yesterday
appeared a year ago. It seemed impossible to
him that so short a distance, so brief a space of
time, divided him from the city where he had but
the day before seen Margaret stepping on board
the little steamer, supported by Philip's arm.
The thought which had yesterday tortured him,
he now smiled at. The cool forest breeze had

blown the mists of the city from his eyes (thus he reasoned), and now he knew that Margaret loved him! How could he doubt it? Had he not felt that she belonged to him from the hour when they had danced together, had breathed the perfume of the same flowers, and felt the same irresistible influence of the spring thrilling in their veins? Had he not heard her love in the low cry she gave that night when he exonerated his friend and acknowledged that it was his hand which had shed the blood of Fernand Thoron? Had he not seen it in the drooping lines of her lithe body as she stood, all white and quivering, as if she had been struck with a mortal blow? He had hesitated long enough; he would go and woo and win the woman he loved. He would pursue her as arduously as ever Indian lover pursued his fleeing bride. He *would* have her for his own. What power in the world was so strong as the passion in his breast? Love, that had o'erturned an empire, was it not strong enough to conquer this girl who mocked him and called him a savage?

He was speaking his thoughts aloud now, while he paced up and down the narrow clearing. On the same spot where the priest had breathed his fervent apostrophe to Nature, Robert paused, and raising his arms above his head, cried with a voice deep as the sound of the sea: "I will have her for my own ; she is mine, mine, mine ! "

A branch rustled near him, and putting aside the leaves, the priest joined his friend. The old man's holy face was very pale, his eyes shone with the brilliancy of youth. What thoughts had the words of this boisterous lover raised in his heart ? He laid his thin hand on the young man's shoulder and said in a faint, low voice, which contrasted as strangely with the full tones that had just now echoed in the forest as did his tall, emaciated body with the powerful frame beside him : " She *shall* be thine ; and when she is dead or faithless, come to me, or if my release has been granted, come to my forest for consolation."

16

CHAPTER XV.

THE balsam of the pine-trees, the quiet of the woods, failed to content for long the child who had so often found consolation and peace in his forest home. The burning fire in his heart parched his whole being. Back to the city he must go ; the Indians could not cheer him, as they had so often done in times past. The priest, whose simple life he had shared so happily in other days, had no words of counsel now to help him. What did *he* know of love and its fierce pain, he whose life had been vowed to the worship of an immaculate goddess? Back to the city, where is no peace, no song of bird, no soft footstep of hidden wood-creature! His feet would fain tread the burning streets again because they led to her dwelling ; while the odorous aisles strewn with pine-needles lose themselves in lonely thickets, fit only for happy lovers or for men wedded to their own thoughts !

After a short visit, the briefest he had ever made them, Robert left the village of his Indian friends and set his face towards the city. He

took leave of the holy man just at nightfall, and
made his way through the woods, guided by the
familiar indications on the trees. It was a breathless night; the stars looked far away and dim
beside one blazing planet that hung low in the
horizon over the city. Never had he seen that
queen of planets so bright. She shone forth
with a mellow radiance, beside which the young
moon looked pale and chilly in comparison. At
a point where three paths converged, the wayfarer stopped, and falling on his knees, held up
his hands adoring, beseeching the point of yellow
flame which shone down upon New Orleans.

His lips moved. Could he be praying to the
evening star, or was he apostrophizing the Love
it typifies? Ere his journey was half accomplished, the star had set; but would it not rise
on the morrow? Early in the morning he
reached the city, having walked since sunset.
The streets were quiet; and foot-weary as he
was, he yielded to the temptation of looking
upon his maiden's dwelling before he went to
rest. The little house looked very friendly.
The blinds of the lower rooms were open, and
his eyes sought the corner where Margaret was
wont to sit of an evening with her small tea-
table beside her. All was as he had last seen
it. With a light step he passed to the garden,
and finding the studio-door unlocked, entered

the familiar room.   There lay her apron as she
had left it, thrown over a chair.   He had the
little blue garment, which still showed the impress of a rounded shoulder, in his arms in
an instant, and kissed it passionately.

Now that he was so near her, he could not go
away without looking upon her face.   The hunger in him for sight and sound and touch of her
was stronger than aught beside.   He would wait,
and while waiting he would sleep a little ; it was
early yet, and he was passing weary.   There was
no couch in the room, and he stretched himself
upon a tiger-skin on the floor, and was asleep
ere he could have counted six of his own heart-
beats.

As he slept, a strange dream came to him.
He was aware of a creature bending over
him, at once as beautiful and as deadly as
the tiger on whose skin he lay.   Through his
heavily closed lids the malignant light of two
strange red-brown eyes seemed to burn into
his brain, a warm breath passed over his face.
He stirred in his sleep and tried to open his
eyes.   In vain!   A voice low and musical as the
murmur of his forest pine-trees chanted words
whose sound alone reached him in the distant
sleep-world : "And the sins of the fathers shall
be visited upon the children.   Do you hear me ?
It is not I who do this thing, but the avenger.

How beautiful you are, Robert! I could almost love you, were it not forbidden." The words ceased ; a faint perfume was wafted over him ; some one had kissed him as he slept, — a kiss burning, yet tender. He had dreamed of such kisses before ; but those dream-embraces were given by a pale maiden with a small rose mouth like a half-unfolded flower, not by this tall woman with fiery dark eyes and lips as red as blood who was now kneeling beside him.

With an effort he awoke and started to his feet, confused and terrified, only to fall back faint and sick, a sharp pain in his side, a cry of agony on his lips. He had been stabbed ; and on the floor beside him lay a jewelled crystal dagger, whose rubies looked pale beside the crimson dye that stained it. He had been stabbed, and he must die unless that red tide creeping across the tiger-skin could be stanched. Beside him was the little blue garment ; he had slept with it in his embrace. With his last remaining strength he pressed the vesture of the woman he loved close to the gaping wound ; and then his very soul seemed to be borne away on the stream of scarlet life-blood creeping across the tiger-skin toward the door.

Nearer and nearer to the sill stole the narrow thread of scarlet liquor, every drop of which lessened his chances of life. It stopped at the

threshold and widened into a little pool, and
lay there sparkling in the light of the sun that
shone alike on flower and tree, on clear falling
fountain, on singing-bird, and on the stricken,
bleeding man. ·

·   ·   ·   ·   ·   ·   ·   ·

Philip Rondelet was a light sleeper, and the
man who had come to rouse him had need to
knock but once, though it was just the hour of
sunrise, when he was wont to sleep most soundly.
His visitor proved to be the *dago*, the half-
brother of Therese's mother. He shambled into
the room through the door which Philip held half
open, and stated his errand. Therese had been
wilder than ever of late ; her mother believed her
mad, but he himself knew better. She had made
a promise to the dead; and those who make prom-
ises to the dead are never easy till they have
kept their word. The man nodded at Philip as if
confident that he was understood, and then went
on with his story. They had watched her till they
were both weary, and the night before she had escaped them, " taking that which she always car-
ries *here* with her," he added, significantly striking
his breast and making a gesture as of stabbing.
The mother had sought her everywhere. They
had been to *his* house, and learned that she had
passed that way, and talked with the servants
of where she might find *him*. They knew not

where else to seek her. Monsieur was *his* friend. Perhaps it would be well if he should warn him ? Mad or not, the girl was a dangerous creature. It was an ill day when she had come back to them with her foreign ways and ideas of being a lady, — a lady, and too good to live and eat with her own flesh and blood !

As he ceased speaking, the man gave an ugly laugh and smote his red cap upon his knee with an angry gesture.

As he listened to the man's story, Philip hastily dressed himself, and by the time the *dago* had finished, he was ready. They went out together, a strangely contrasted pair, the tall and graceful figure of Rondelet, aristocratic in out-, line, exquisite in dress, towering above the short, heavily-built plebeian, strong and stupid as an ox. By that subtler sense of intuition he knew where to seek Robert ; and while he was making all speed to reach and warn him, a suggestion floated through his mind whose baseness was only realized in the moment when it was indignantly dismissed, — " Why should he interfere ? Why should he step out of his way to warn his rival of a possible danger, of a fate which he perhaps deserved ? "

He shuddered as he understood the full meaning of that whispered temptation, and was thankful to see by the unabated pace of his companion that his feet had not faltered one instant on their errand of warning.

So it is that to the most noble, to the most white-souled of men, come thoughts of evil, promptings of the lower nature. It is not, as unwilling sinners would fain believe, that the good are so by nature and without effort ; it is that they have strength to strangle the evil thought before it becomes a deed, to tear out the base desire and cast it from them before it is fulfilled.

All was quiet at Margaret's dwelling, no sign of life about the house or garden. His imagination, without doubt, had tricked him. The flowers bloomed serenely, the bird in the magnolia-tree twittered to her little ones, and the cat, sunning herself under the piazza rail, rubbed her nose against his legs in friendly greeting. The studio door stood ajar. He stepped quickly over the threshold ; his foot slipped on something shiny and treacherous, and as he saved himself from falling, he saw lying before him the form of his friend Robert Feuardent, his face white and set with the look of death. The *dago* saw all this too, and one thing more, — a small dagger, which glistened in the light and broke the sunbeams into splinters of colors more splendid than the rarest gems. He hid the weapon in his breast, with a watchful glance at Philip to see whether the action was observed ; but the physician either did not see or purposely ignored what the other had done, his attention being riveted on the man so grievously in need of his utmost skill. As with the aid of his rough companion Philip busied himself over the wounded man, his thoughts reverted to a scene not unlike this one. He half expected to see the face of Jean Thoron, of his young colleague, of Therese, beside him as he turned from the wounded man ; but he was alone with the *dago*.

There was one more point of difference in the case, — Fernand Thoron had been doomed to die from the first, and the man who had killed him had one chance of life left.

CHAPTER XVI.

IF one must be ill at all, the Hôtel-Dieu is a pleasant place to be ill in. It stands back from the street; a stretch of cool green turf, shaded by manifold trees and sweetened by innumerable flowers, lying between it and the dusty thoroughfare. Looking between the bars of the high-grated gate, one may catch a glimpse of the interior, where light-footed sisters of mercy glide from room to room, ministering to the sick who are so fortunate as to come under their gentle care. Late one afternoon, perhaps a week from the day when Robert Feuardent had been brought to the hospital senseless and wounded nigh unto death, his friend and physician rang at the gate. From the dark interior came two white-coifed nuns passing down the wide steps and along the flagged path to admit him.

"How is he this evening?" he asked anxiously, as the elder sister, taking a key from her girdle, unlocked the gate.

" He has been worrying himself almost into a fever, calling for you; but his head is quite clear, I think."

"Philip, how long you have been!" cried the sufferer impatiently, as Rondelet entered the small room where he lay, the one vivid thing in the white and spotless cell.

"I am sorry, Robert, I could not come sooner; but you are so much better, you really do not need me," Rondelet said gently.

"I need you more than ever, for I have something to say to you."

The physician shook his head and touched his patient's wrist; but Robert would not be denied.

"Philip, dear Philip," he cried, "let me talk to you to-night! I must tell you something that weighs upon me."

Another repetition! Save that it was a man's face lying flushed and pain-racked among the pillows, a man's voice that pleaded with him, Philip felt that he might have been reacting the scene of weeks ago, when Therese had told him the story of her wrongs and grief. He was so startled by the vivid recollection that for the moment he said nothing, and only took his friend's hot hand in both of his.

"Philip, if I die — and I know that I may die — promise me that you will tell Margaret Ruysdale the secret I am going to confide to you now."

"I promise."

Rondelet felt a foreknowledge of what was coming; he was as sure as that he lived that he was to hear more of the story of Therese than she had ever told him. The last link in the chain was to be supplied; he was to learn what bond there was between Robert and Therese that had made the man so merciful and forbearing, the woman so full of pitiless hatred.

"You remember the day when those bloodhounds were here, wearying me with their questions?" the patient continued.

"Yes."

"I told them that I did not know who struck me. It was a lie; you knew it was a lie when I spoke it. I saw that you knew as well as if you had seen her, who it was that struck the blow."

Philip bowed his head in assent.

"Yes, it was she, Therese," Robert went on eagerly; "and because she is a woman and heedless, and because the bloodhounds are keen of scent, they will track her, and it will be known that I fell by her hand. You must save her; and when she is safe, you must go to Margaret and tell her all. She knows half the story; it is not fair that she should not hear the rest. No, do not wait; tell her to-night. Therese is the cause of all this misery, and yet I must protect her; for — Philip, come closer — I swore to my father on his death-bed that I would shield her

always — because — he — my father, was her
father, and because, before God, she is my
sister."

"Your sister?"

"Yes, my sister. Her mother — you have
seen her — is half Spanish, half negro; she
belonged to my father."

"Therese your sister!" repeated Philip. "I
thought she was—" he hesitated.

"My mistress? Ay, and so does the rest of
the world; it may be that Margaret thinks this
thing of me."

"Now I begin to understand it all," said Philip.
"You tried to separate her from Thoron?"

"Yes," interrupted Robert; "how could I see
her openly disgraced and brought to shame?
She was gently bred, reared like a lady, in
ignorance of what she was. If she had been
my own sister she could not have been more
tenderly nurtured. I strove to induce her to
leave him. She would not listen to me, and
appealed to him; in the quarrel that ensued, he
forced me to fight. You know the rest well
enough."

"Yes," said Philip, speaking slowly and gravely,
"yes, I know it all; and I know that with his
dying breath Fernand Thoron called upon that
woman to bear witness that the fault was his
alone, and that you were not to blame."

"He said that? Swear to me that you are telling the truth!"

"I have never lied in my life."

"Philip!" The name died on his lips, and the hand that clasped Rondelet's grew cold. Robert had fainted. He came to his senses only to fall into a deep sleep; and Philip, as he watched him, was convinced that the corner was turned, and that the morning would see his patient out of danger.

Before he slept that night Rondelet had a duty ˜to perform, a message to deliver. He stopped at the Ruysdales on his way from the hospital to Jackson Square. Margaret was expecting him. The evening was very warm, and the young girl was sitting on the veranda with her father. Sara Harden and her faithful cavalier, Bouton de Rose, arrived just as Philip came up the steps.

"Ah, Philippe le bel, it is you!" cried Mrs. Harden. "Never were you more welcome than at this moment, — what news of Feuardent?"

Margaret's eyes had already asked the question. .

"He is much better to-night; I think I can almost pronounce him out of danger."

"There's no killing a fellow like that," said Bouton de Rose. "He is a Hercules. What a physique, what muscles! A gladiator!"

" Yes ; there's a great deal of him to kill," said Mrs. Harden, dryly.

When she found that Robert was in a fair way to recover, her womanly compassion was forgotten, and her old prejudice against Philip's rival came back.

" What a tragic year this has been ! " she continued ; " enough of melodrama to fill a five-act play. I think it very vulgar and third-rate, all this blood and murder and detectives. One is obliged to know so much about it all, too, in this country. They manage these things better in France, do they not, Comte ? "

" Ah ! madame is always so amiable in her recollections of my country."

" Because it's my country too, and Mr. Rondelet's also. Paris belongs to the world, not only to the French. Is it not so Philip ? You are at heart more of a Frenchman than an American."

" I certainly was once, Mrs. Harden. To-day I cannot say. I feel very differently about my own country."

" *Tiens !* This *is* a change of base. Why, six months ago I heard you declare, — I remember your very words, — ' I would give my life for this country, because it would be my duty to do so ; I would die for France because I love her.' "

" That was the expression of a momentary enthusiasm," said the Count. " Besides, what could be more natural? M. Rondelet is French in name, in blood, — is it not so? — largely even by education. *Allez !* it is most natural, he is more than half a Frenchman. I have always claimed you as a compatriot, *mon cher."*

"·Yes," said Mrs. Harden with a sigh, — she was unaccountably depressed this evening, — " Philip *is* changed. He once had time to read with me, to walk with me, to sing with me, to be, in short, a little companionable ; now he has taken up his profession, and my husband tells me he is the hardest worked doctor in town. What 's the use of working? I hate work ; but the provoking thing is that you working people are always the most amusing, while idlers like myself are very boresome to me. It 's a hard old world."

Margaret laughed as she had not laughed for a week, and patted her friend's soft hand, saying, —

" You work too hard in trying to amuse yourself ; there is no harder work than that in the world."

" Now, Margaret, no philosophy, please. 'Out of the mouths of babes and sucklings' is all very well ; but from a chit like you I can't endure it. Come, Comte, I must get back to my old Gaffer

Harden ; it is ten o'clock and after. Good-night all. Go to bed early, Madge ; you are losing your color from keeping too late hours. Philip, you never come to the house now ; I want to see you soon. General, is it too late for you to walk part of the way with us ? I want to consult you about my " — she hesitated a moment — " about my — my new picture-gallery. You know I think of building an extension this summer."

With a smile as innocent as that of a child she looked into the old General's face and carried him off triumphantly, a willing slave to her charms. The wily enchantress discoursed for an hour with that innocent man about her imaginary picture-gallery, to the astonishment of good Darius Harden, who was too diplomatic a soul and too well-disciplined a husband to betray any surprise at the startling plans which his wife was now disclosing for the first time.

Meanwhile Philip was left alone with Margaret after the long, hard day's work, which jarred upon his artistic, sensitive nature more than even she, who knew him so well, could guess. His passionate love of beautiful things in nature and in art made each ugly and diseased being that came under his care a positive pain to him ; yet he had endured this for her sake, that he might be more worthy of her. Had he not earned the right to speak, to tell her what he had done for her, to

sue for that love which was the only reward life
held for him ?   He was very weary ; he longed
to speak ; and yet one thought kept him silent, —
his promise to Feuardent.   He had sworn to tell
her that very night the story of which she knew
but the outside facts.

She seemed conscious of the struggle in his
breast, for she suddenly turned to him and bade
him tell her what was troubling him.   He was
still silent.

"I am sure it is something about Mr. Feuardent that you have to say."

"Yes, my child, you are right ; you are always
right.   I have something to tell you from Robert,
— a message, a story, I hardly know which."

" Let it be a story, you tell them so well."

And so he spoke, and told the story as he was
gifted to do, with a concentrated earnestness
and a repressed eloquence that held his listener
breathless and expectant.   It is a great gift that
of the *raconteur*.   In Italy it is considered a
talent of the highest order, and is cultivated as
carefully as a tenor voice.   In that favored land
the speech of the *improvvisatore* flows in rhymed
numbers ; but the greatest master of that rare art
never had a more entranced listener than had
Philip Rondelet as he told the story of Therese,
of Fernand, and of Robert to Margaret.   We
all enjoy doing the things that we do well ;

and forgetting everything but his auditor and his theme, Philip soon broke from the measured sentences with which he began the recital, and with an almost Oriental grace and richness of speech painted for Margaret the various scenes of the story in which he had participated or which had been described to him.

Fascinated by the narrative, magnetized by the speaker, Margaret sat looking into Philip's face with a rapt attention which might well have deceived a more shrewd observer than himself. Was it wonderful the lover believed that the look she gave him as she laid in his hand the breast-knot she had worn that night was love-laden ?

He caught her hand in his own and raised it, trembling all the while at his own temerity, to his lips; and Margaret did not frown, but gently drew it from him as a step sounded upon the walk and her father joined them.

The General had come just five minutes too soon ! There was nothing to do but to take leave, and with a light step Philip left the house and made his way to Jackson Square. His tiny apartment, " on the first story down the chimney," as he was wont to call it, was cool and sweet with the spray of the little fountain. The windows were wide open, and a single flower spread its scented heart to the beauty of the night. But once in the year this aged cactus blossomed, and on this white night, the happiest in all Philip Rondelet's life, the cereus had bloomed for him. The delicate waxen petals slowly unfolded, revealing the deep heart which seemed to glow with a hidden flame. The perfume, unlike that of any other flower, floated about him like an incense. As he kept his vigil with the wondrous blossom, it seemed to him that the eyes of his soul were looking into a heart as fresh and fragrant. He believed that he could see the light of love burning for him, faint and tender as the mystic radiance of the cereus. Margaret loved him. For the first time he believed that his heart's desire was granted. She loved him. Why else should she have smiled so happily in his face? Why had she talked with him in the old, unreserved way that had been hers ere the cloud had come between them? Why had she, with that inimitable gesture of grace and shyness, taken the flowers from her breast and laid them in his hand, letting her own linger while he kissed the little palm till it was pink with blushes? Margaret loved him; and happy in that belief after the long doubt and fear, dismissed now forever, he fell asleep.

With the morrow came his daily tasks and the remembrance of that other promise he had made Robert, to find Therese and save her from the

creatures of the law. Where should he begin
the search ? It seemed an almost hopeless one.
Her mother and uncle denied all knowledge of
her. She had vanished, they said, leaving no
trace behind. He could not communicate with
the police authorities without strengthening the
suspicions already entertained by them. Hero
was his only confidant, and all that day the two
men searched for the desperate woman, each in
his own way. Philip failed to find Margaret at
the studio when he called. He was grieved at
this, but he felt confident that he should see her
that evening. He would then tell her of the
wealth of love in his heart, — hers, all hers, —
more than ever woman was blessed with before.

And Margaret, unconscious of the hope and
joy which she had given him, thought only of the
story he had told her the night before and of the
man who was its hero. For the first time in
many days she went cheerfully about her household tasks, ordered her father's dinner, and su-
perintended the house-work ; and when Philip
came, trembling with hope and love, to see her,
she was in the kitchen making broth for Robert
Feuardent. The sympathetic servant-maid who
opened the door had compassion on his eager
face, and instead of giving the curt " too much
engaged to receive any one," told him smilingly
that " Miss Ruysdale had gone out early with

the General." Margaret was full of kindliness that day, and the little children who came begging at her gate went away full-handed and rejoicing. She had a smile, one of her rare smiles, for every creature who crossed her path on that sunny spring morning; and when she at last went to her work in the studio, her voice vied with that of the bird in the magnolia-tree in melody and joy.

Just before sundown Margaret left the house, carrying on her arm a basket containing the can of broth she had watched that day with an interest which she had never before felt regarding any culinary operation. She took the road the bearers had chosen on the morning when Robert Feuardent had been carried to the Hôtel-Dieu, the quickest and quietest route, one which Philip Rondelet had traversed many a day on his way to and from the work he had undertaken for love of her. She walked bravely and swiftly for the first half of the way; but as she drew near the hospital her pace slackened and her heart beat fast with excitement. The building was now in sight. With a heightened color and a perfectly oblivious expression she passed the gate and turned down the next street, as if she had no more interest in the place than the first-comer. Near at hand there was a small square, with a few shade-trees and some wooden benches. Here

she sat down, and with the point of her parasol
drew an intricate design in the soft earth of the
path. When it was carefully finished she quickly
obliterated it with her foot, and then repeated the
drawing, enlarging the outline a little. It was
still unsatisfactory, and this time the lines seemed
shorter and less vigorous. A yellow dog of an
ungenteel appearance now joined her, and after
vainly trying to decipher the hieroglyphics Margaret was tracing, turned his attention to the
basket, from which proceeded a savory odor.
Recalled to herself by this impertinent and un-
warrantable curiosity on the part of the yellow
dog, Miss Ruysdale suddenly rose, and with a
firm step and severe expression of countenance
again approached the Hôtel-Dieu. This time she
got as far as the gate, and with a trembling hand
rang the bell. The door of the hall flew open
and the guardian of the gate descended, alone
this time, the visitor being of the female sex.

"I want to see Sister Gabrielle," Margaret
said, in a voice that would not be quite firm;
"I have brought something for one of the
patients."

"Enter, my child," said the sister kindly, "and
I will find Sister Gabrielle for you."

In the long, severe waiting-room, with its religious engravings and library of the lives of the
saints, Margaret Ruysdale, sculptor, the com-

posed and serious young woman, sat trembling and blushing as any other foolish girl might have done.   When the grave gray-eyed Sister Gabrielle swept into her presence, stately and imposing in her serge frock as she had been in her state robes when she presided over one of the great houses of the Faubourg St. Germain, Margaret's courage gave out entirely, and she faltered: " I came to ask about — Dr. Rondelet has often spoken to me of you.   I — I am Miss Ruysdale. I brought some broth, and I want to know how Mr. Feuardent is."

" Mademoiselle Risdelle ? Ah, yes." The dignity had melted from Sister Gabrielle's face ; there was only a tender kindliness now.   " Ah, I know you vare well, mademoiselle.   I have to thank you on account of many, many gracious gifts at my patients," — she spoke English with apparent effort.   " But you spik French, don't it ?   *Enfin, c'est mieux ;* " and relapsing into her mother tongue, she made Margaret heartily welcome to the hospital, and gave her a full and satisfactory account of the patient's condition.

" He is asleep now," said the sister as Margaret rose to go.   " Would you not like to look into the room and to see how comfortable he is ? "

Margaret bowed.   She could not speak, but followed the sister down the wide cool passage to an open door.

" Ah, the soup ! I had forgotten it," whispered Sister Gabrielle innocently. " Wait here till I bring you the basket and the can."

She was gone, and Margaret was left alone on the threshold of the small airy room. It was now nearly dark ; but the fading light from the window showed the narrow white bed. Margaret could dimly discern a face among the pillows. The regular breathing showed that the patient was asleep. The girl shivered with a new and acute pain, and yielding to a desire whose force she had no strength to combat, she stole noiselessly across the threshold, and by slow degrees reached the bedside. She stood looking down at the pale handsome face lying there in the gray twilight. So quietly had she moved that the watcher, drowsing in the easy-chair in the shadow of the door, was not aware of her presence till with a low sigh and a sudden raising of her hands to her heart Margaret bent her fair proud head and touched the sleeper's forehead with her lips.

Robert Feuardent had been kissed for a second time as he slept ; but the light caress of the maiden lips which laid their first kiss upon his brow only soothed him to a deeper, happier slumber. Like a rosy shadow, Margaret stole from that dim room and flew down the corridor and out into the streets, her basket, the nun

— all else forgotten in that blissful tumult of pain and pleasure which she now knew to be Love, —

> " For we knew thee mother of life,
> But knew thee not mother of death ! "

When Sister Gabrielle returned with the basket, she found her visitor fled, and instead of the trembling girl she had left on the threshold, the tall figure of Philip Rondelet, who had sat watching his friend's slumber that afternoon from the arm-chair in the shadow of the doorway.

" You are going, Doctor ? "

" Yes, he is doing well. There is no change to be made in the treatment. I shall not be back again to-night. Good-by."

The Doctor's voice sounded a little strangely, the sister thought, and his pale face and deep eyes wore an expression she had never seen in them before. " He is overworked," she said to herself. " There is more of the spirit than the flesh about that man, or he could not endure what he does."

The Doctor's face haunted the nun that night, and she added a prayer for the peace of his soul to the long list of requirements which in a perfect, childlike faith she sent up to the ever-gracious and accessible Mother of God.

CHAPTER XVII.

AFTER leaving the Hôtel-Dieu, Philip Rondelet repaired to the club where it was his habit
to dine. He took his accustomed seat, and mechanically perused the evening paper which the
servant placed beside his plate. It is presumable
that he ate his dinner; it is certain that the
usual number of courses were placed before him,
and the same quantity of wine. If the waiter
had been called upon to testify as to Mr. Rondelet's condition that evening, it is probable that he
would have remarked that the gentleman seemed
"absent-like," and took little note of what he
ate; that he chose his cigar without noticing the
brand, and omitted to light it as he walked out
of the club. If Philip had been ordered to give
an account of himself between the time of his
leaving the hospital and the hour when he found
himself in his room staring at his own face in
the mirror, he would have found it an impossible
task. A perfect blank had settled upon him, —
a numbness of heart and brain merciful, but,
alas! only too brief.

It had seemed to him that he was a ship-wrecked man alone in mid-ocean, seated on a single rock o'ertopping the waves. All about him were the smooth green waters lapping the rock and gently laving his feet. It was very hot, the sun blazed down upon him ; and yet he felt no present pain, only a terror of what was to come. The shriek of the sea-mew sounded in his ears — it was but the sweet voice of his caged ringdove cooing to him — and a foul carrion-bird flapped its wings as it circled slowly about him ; still no pain, only a growing appre-hension as the sea-water, grown hot and biting, rose about the rock, rippling against his knees with a sound as of faint diabolic laughter. Higher and higher rose the flood, till hip and breast and chin were covered ; and ah ! at last he had found his voice. As the bitter water rushed into his mouth he gave a strangling cry and started to his feet, to find himself alone in his apartment, his own haggard face, reflected in the mirror, the only thing of all that fearful vision that remained. Then came "remembrance risen from hell," and he cried out again ; but this time his voice was sharp with sorrow only, the terror born of the moment's madness was passed.

"Margaret ! Margaret !" he cried, "how could you deceive me so ? False ! false ! false ! Like

all other women, born only to snare and tor-
ture ! "

He clasped his hot hands together and wrung
them mercilessly ; he struck his forehead with
his clenched hand, moved by that strange instinct which seeks to divert a mental agony by
inflicting a physical pain half as intense.

But his rage was of short duration ; there
was more of grief than of anger in him, — that
grief which gnaws at the heart-strings and saps
strength and hope, and finally life itself. He
loved her too well, too purely, to hold his anger.
Sister Gabrielle had spoken truly when she said,
"there is more of the spirit than of the flesh
about the man." The red flush faded from his
brow and cheek, and left him pale and cold with
the mortal chilliness of despair. There was no
hope ; Margaret loved another. Life, which had
looked so bright that morning, was insupporta-
ble now. He could not bear the thought that
seemed to blend spirit and flesh into one ceaseless agony, vibrating through his being with
every beat of the heart. He could not bear it !
Reason itself would be consumed in that fierce
struggle ; rather let it be life ! The instant the
thought struck him he started to his feet, and
from his medicine-chest drew forth a small phial
containing a deadly drug. Five drops would suf-
fice to ease the feverish pain throbbing in every

nerve and braih-cell. With a steady hand he poured the clear, colorless liquid into a medicine-glass, accurately measuring the dose and replacing the stopper from force of habit. He raised the glass, it already touched his lips, when he paused, seemed to hesitate, and then put the glass down with a low sigh.

" Therese — I had forgotten my promise ; well, this can wait."

He poured the drops carefully back into the phial, crushed the glass beneath his heel, and then, locking the door behind him, went downstairs into the street.

Where to find that mad girl, that would-be murderess ? he asked himself again and again. His whole mind was fixed as intently upon finding Therese as it had been just now on his own destruction. Until he found her he could not be at rest. He had given his word to save her, and with that word unredeemed he could not sleep at ease in his grave. Where to find her ? He had exhausted all the places where there was any probability of hearing of her, he was at a loss what to do next. Meanwhile, his feet had brought him to the river-side ; he stood leaning against a pier. Presently he laughed aloud at a thought that passed through his mind.

"I cannot even die till I have found and

saved Robert Feuardent's bastard sister! Ye
gods, there's something grotesque about that!"

Where should he look for her? That was the
thought that puzzled him as he stood there in
the shadow of the pier meditating his plan of
action, while the mighty river, quiet and resist-
less in its silent strength, flowed swiftly by the
city lying in its cool embrace. He was quite
unconscious of the passage of time, and the
clock on the cathedral in Jackson Square rang
out the hours without attracting his attention.
It must have been somewhere about midnight
when he was roused from the revery into which
he had fallen. He was startled by something
rustling past him as he stood leaning against
the wooden pier. In an instant his senses were
keenly alert. It was a woman's dress that
had touched him; he was sure of that — yes —
there was the woman now, sitting a few paces
from him on the edge of the bank. She seemed
very tired, for she had chosen a place where
some logs of wood made a support for her, and
she leaned back, rolling up her cloak to form a
cushion for her head. Philip felt a movement of
compassion for this homeless creature who had
no other resting-place than a pile of lumber on
the levee. He felt in his pocket: he had some
money with him; it might help this wanderer,
and it would be pleasant to think that he had

made one human being less wretched before he was admitted to the great calm. He was about to approach her, when the woman suddenly rose and walked rapidly to the brink of the river. She took her cloak, and drawing from her breast some small articles which he could not distinguish, knotted them in its folds and threw the bundle into the water. In an instant it was whirled away by the swift current. The woman watched the senseless thing swirling in the strong tide, and gave a low cry, as if the sight were painful to her.

"I wish I had not done that," he heard her say in an undertone, "it looks so horrible."

Philip, dimly understanding the import of the scene, had drawn unobserved close behind the woman. She could not make a movement which he could not check. The moon, which had been obscured, now broke through a mass of purple cloud, its light transforming the sombre river into an argent tide and making the dark river-bank as bright as day. It showed to Philip Rondelet the graceful outline of the figure before him. She shuddered at the sight of the moon, and muffling her head and face more closely in the folds of the lace mantilla which she wore, she made a sudden movement, throwing her arms above her head, as if to leap into the river. A strong arm was thrown about her, and she was drawn struggling back from the perilous edge.

"Wretched woman! what are you doing?"

"Drowning myself; and by what right do you dare to stop me? Cannot one die in peace in this accursed city?" she cried. She had ceased to struggle with him.

Philip stood between her and the river, his hand upon her arm.

"One may die in peace, but one may not take one's own life; it is forbidden."

"By whom?"

"It is against the law of God and of man."

"And what are you who dare to stop me?"

What was he indeed, and by what right did he, the would-be suicide of an hour ago, endeavor to turn this poor girl from her bent?

"Don't you know me, Therese?"

She looked at him, and then the rage died from her face. She fell upon her knees at his feet and clasped his hand in both of hers, crying imploringly: "It is you, then! *You* are my friend, my only friend in this great city, where I am hunted like a dog. Let me die! let me die! What have I to live for?"

He could not answer her; knowing her miserable story, how could he — he of all men on God's earth that night — tell her why she must live and suffer when peace was so near at hand beneath the river? For one brief moment he faltered; the thought came to him of taking this broken-hearted, sinful creature by the hand and leaping with her into the flood. But the moment passed, the temptation was overcome, and he lifted his voice and spoke to the kneeling, weeping woman, about whose desperate beauty the moonlight played fancifully. He spoke to her as only those who are gifted with the living speech can speak,—words which can no more be written down and read again than can the subtle power which animates them be prisoned and made material. Those who have heard the sentences of one of these seers among men never forget what they felt in hearing and answering them. For it is their gift to appeal to the best and noblest thoughts in men's hearts, howsoever deeply these thoughts may be buried under sin and selfishness. The hidden water for which men thirst lies in the depths of their own souls, and the living word is the divining-rod which points out its source, so oft forgotten or ignored.

And when he was at last silent, and the weeping woman had risen and laid her hand in his and bade him do with her as he would, the man knew that the battle had been fought and won for her, and eke for him. And so it is that we are sometimes preserved from falling into a sin by the act of saving another from the very snare into which we were walking, open-eyed and unashamed.

The night had grown chilly ; Therese was shivering in the piercing river-breeze. What was he to do with her? Where could she find shelter at that hour? It was past one o'clock. She must be housed until the morning, when he would get her away from the city.

Sara Harden — she would help him in this strait, and keep the secret of the unfortunate who now clung trembling to his arm.

" Come, Therese, let us walk fast ; you are half numb with the damp air."

Mrs. Harden was one of those people who have an inborn prejudice against daylight, preferring the night for pleasure, for thought, and for social intercourse. Philip had not reckoned without his hostess when he had decided to claim her hospitality for the weary creature whose footsteps he supported through the deserted streets. There was a light in the music-room of Darius Harden's house. The blind was partly ajar, and through the window Philip could distinguish a slight figure reclining in a great chair near the reading-table. All the rest of the house was dark. At the risk of startling the little woman he tapped gently on the window and said in a low voice : " Mrs. Harden, it is I, Rondelet ; don't be frightened."

The arm-chair was suddenly upset, and a small white figure with loosened hair rushed to the window.

"Philip! What brings you here at this hour? Is anything wrong?"

"Open the window, dear friend, and let us in. I have brought some one who needs shelter badly."

"You are not alone, then?" cautiously.

"No; I have brought you a poor girl half frozen, half starved."

The window flew open, and the impulsive soul caught Therese by the arm and drew her from the dark street into the dainty little boudoir, all light and flowers and perfume. She placed the girl in her own chair, not forgetting to toss out of sight, before its title caught Philip's eyes, the yellow-covered French novel she had been reading. He smiled as he marked the action, and said: "I was almost certain of finding you up still. May she stay here for a few hours? Let her lie on the sofa till morning. I shall come for her before your people are stirring."

"Of course she shall stay," answered Sara Harden warmly. "Poor child, she looks so ill! Are you not hungry? Wait till I bring you something to eat."

She bustled out of the room, and Philip, kneeling upon the hearth, blew the embers into a blaze.

Now that the full light fell upon her, he saw how terribly Therese had changed since he had last seen her. Her face had paled to the color of alabaster, and her sombre eyes were sunken and hollow. The warmth of the fire, the effect of the food and wine of which Sara Harden urged her to partake, soon brought a shade of color to her cheek ; and half an hour after her entrance into that cheerful room the girl's eyes had lost the wild expression which made her look more like a hunted animal than a human being. Philip felt that he had best leave her alone with the tender-hearted lady ; and so, warning her that she must be ready for him at daylight, he left the house.

For an hour he had not thought of himself. Now that he was alone again, his trouble settled down upon him like a heavy pall. Yet his spirit did not quail under it. Strength had come to him, and he had manfully shouldered the burden of grief laid upon him. He reached his room and sat down to think what he had best do with Therese, what he could do for himself. The events of the day came back to him, and he reviewed them coolly and dispassionately, as if he had been but an on-looker of his own grief and madness. He recalled every incident, from the moment when he had left the hospital to that which saw him sitting in the gray morning twi-

light under the leads of the old Pontalba Building. By a curious action of the brain he remembered things which had made no impression on
his mind at the moment they occurred, — the
dinner he had tried to eat at the club, the paper
he had feigned to read, the words of the despatch
which he had perused, but whose import he had
not till now comprehended : —

"TO THE PEOPLE OF NEW ORLEANS : Send us help !
The fever has broken out. People are dying by hun-
dreds. Doctors and nurses are needed.

"THEBES."

Thebes, a sister city in a neighboring State, a
city bound to New Orleans by the closest ties of
affection and sympathy, cried to her for help in
her hour of agony !

Philip Rondelet started to his feet as the words
of the despatch flashed through his brain. His
resolve was taken in that moment ; and before
the sun had risen he had completed his preparations for the journey that lay before him.

Therese was awaiting him. The few hours
which she had passed in the society of a woman
who had treated her with the simple and unques-
tioning politeness which is an essential of good
breeding, had transformed the wild outcast of
the night into a quiet, dignified woman who met
the man who had but a few hours ago saved her

life with a half smile sadder than tears. Was
this the same Therese that he had heard swear-
ing vengeance on her brother's head over her
dead lover's body ? Was this the fever-stricken
woman who had poured into his ears the story
of her broken life, — the would-be suicide he had
saved from the river's fierce tide ? Had she, in
truth, been maddened by her grief, and was he
seeing for the first time the real Therese in
this dignified and beautiful woman ? He asked
himself these questions as he looked at her, little
guessing that in himself had lain the power which
had wrought the wonderful transformation.

Sara Harden was waiting for him too, very
pale and pretty in her soft white morning wrap-
per. She asked him no question, though she
saw the carriage at the door laden with his
luggage.

He took her hand and said : " Dear friend,
good-by. Thank you for what you have done
for — for mademoiselle ; she will never forget it,
I am sure. I am going to put her on the steamer
which sails in an hour for France, and then I am
going, — it is right that you should know, — I
am going to Thebes. They have sent a call for
doctors — "

" To Thebes ! " she cried, her face turning
white as her dress. " Philip, do you know that
for you, almost a stranger to this climate, that

means the fever, and the fever means death?
No, no, you cannot go; let others who have
nothing to live for risk their lives — "

He looked at her sadly, and raised her hand
to his lips.

" *You* will miss me ? "

There was an infinite yearning in his face and
voice. The next moment he was gone; and
Sara Harden, burying her fair head in her hands,
sat down and wept as the carriage bore away
toward the pest-stricken town the man whom
she had always loved as a heart's' brother.

At the station there was the usual crowd of
hangers-on, and but few passengers, as it was
still very early. A small, clean-shaven man
leaning against the rail outside the ticket-office
seemed absorbed in studying the labyrinthine
table of outgoing trains. A cab drove up at a
sharp pace, and Philip Rondelet, jumping lightly
to the ground, turned and said in an undertone
to his companion : "Are you in earnest, Therese ?
It is not yet too late for the steamer. For the
last time, will you not give up the idea of going
with me ? "

" No, I am determined. If you can risk your
life, why should I love mine too much to do the
same thing ? "

" It is very different. You are a woman, and
have no knowledge of the work you are under-

taking. As for me, I am a physician, and it is my duty to go where I am needed. Come, my child, give it up. Believe me, it is better for you."

She looked at him, terrified at the thought of leaving him, and shook her head.

" No, I have decided."

Rondelet saw that it was useless to attempt to dissuade her, and after giving Hero orders to attend to the baggage, stepped to the ticket-office.

" Three tickets for Thebes."

" Return ? "

" No, — it's hardly necessary ; they might never be wanted."

The man laughed at the grim jest and handed the tickets to Philip. At this moment the lounger, who had to all appearance never removed his eyes from the table of trains he was studying, greeted Philip.

" Morning, Doctor."

" Ah, Dryer, is that you ? "

" Yes, sir. I am here," he said, lowering his voice, " on the lookout for certain persons whom the authorities prefer to keep in New Orleans."

" You are still on the force then ? " said Philip indifferently. He had recognized in Dryer an old acquaintance and a member of the detective force.

" Yes, sir ; and I beg your pardon for asking

the question, but what is the name of that lady in the carriage ? "

" Really, Dryer, I don't understand by what right — " Philip began angrily.

" I know, sir," the man said apologetically ; " but you see duty is duty, and your friend comes uncommon near to a description I have of a certain woman we are after."

" There 's some mistake, I think.   I have just called for that lady at Darius Harden's house, where she spent last night.   Is it likely now that a friend of mine and of Mrs. Harden can be in any way connected with a matter of the kind you suggest ? "

" I know, Doctor ; but the first rule of my profession is that appearances are deceitful."

" I have no time to lose, Mr. Dryer.   I am on my way to Thebes.   You saw the appeal in last night's paper ?   This lady, who is going as a nurse, is under my care.   Does that satisfy you ? "

" No, sir."

" Ask the driver if what I have said is true."

" Your word, Doctor, is all that I require.   If you will assure me that the lady in the carriage is not a certain Therese Caseneuve, suspected of having assaulted Mr. Robert Feuardent, I shall be satisfied."

Philip changed color.   He would have given

his life to save the woman from this new disgrace ;
but his word !

He looked the little gimlet-eyed detective
fairly in the eyes, and said : " I pledge you my
word of honor that every word I have told you
about that lady is true. She is going to Thebes,
taking her life in her hand, to help those pest-
stricken people ; I will hold myself responsible
for her. And I charge you, as you are a man,
not to challenge a soldier on the way to duty at
a post of danger, it may be of death."

He had laid his hand on the man's shoulder,
and was looking at him with that burning look in
his strange eyes which was wont to control the
men and women who met it.

" Well, Doctor, if you say it 's all right, I must
take your word for it," said the detective, slowly
turning away. " I am afraid I 've let the wool
be pulled over my eyes with those same optics a
leetle too wide open," he added to himself.

By this time the train was ready to start ;
Philip, Therese, and Hero had taken their places.
With a sudden spasm of official remorse, Dryer
rushed to the window of the car where Rondelet
was sitting.

" Doctor, I have your word for the reappearance of that person if she is wanted ? "

" The person will be in the place I told you of ;
but you must come yourself to get her. Good-

by, Dryer.   When you see Mr. Feuardent, tell
him what was said between us."

"Good-by, Dr. Rondelet! good-by, marm!
May the Lord have mercy on them both!" he
added under his breath as the train with its
scanty complement of passengers thundered out
of the depot, laden with medicines, with garments, with food and money for the relief of the
fever-stricken city, for which only three travellers
were booked.

CHAPTER XVIII.

From the day on which Margaret had paid that clandestine visit to the hospital, Robert had steadily improved. Whether there was some hidden efficacy in the broth she had made for him, and which was, if the truth must be told, quite inferior to that prepared under the supervision of Sister Gabrielle, or whether the light touch on his forehead of a pair of trembling lips had wrought the favorable change in his condition, must be left to the imagination of the reader, if he have one; if he have not, he will not trouble himself with either hypothesis, but will take it for granted that it was thanks to his superb constitution that Robert Feuardent's wound healed in such a short space of time.

The sisters had lavished every care on the handsome young man who had proved so agreeable and interesting a patient. They were almost more sorry for themselves than glad for him when the day on which he was to be discharged drew near. Nuns are very human when one gets to know them well, and is no longer awed

by the severity of their black robes; and it is
only human for women, young or old, to prefer
tending a young man full of grace and beauty, to
waiting on some snuffy, cross old fellow, or a fretful, nervous woman. Robert afterwards avowed
that had it not been for a certain image which
always hovered about him, he should have fallen
helplessly in love with the sweet, stately Sister
Gabrielle. They were very pleasant, those days
of convalescence; his friends all came to see
him, even General Ruysdale, who before his illness had treated him with a certain reserve and
caution. Bouton de Rose came at least once a
day, with all the social news of the hour, which
he gathered as quickly and naturally as a bee
gathers honey. The Count, indeed, felt as if
he had found a second home in the Crescent
City. It is a wonderfully hospitable place, New
Orleans, and the stranger who after a three
months' residence there does not feel himself
part and parcel of its society, linked to it by
sympathy and good-will, must be a curmudgeon
indeed.

Robert heard of Philip's departure for Thebes
with a divided feeling. He shuddered to think
of the work that his friend had undertaken, and
yet felt that it was not so hard to be chained
to the hospital when there was no rival near to
Margaret. He sent half of his quarter's income

to his friend for the sick at Thebes and for the comfortable housing of the woman who had gone to nurse them. The money was acknowledged by a brief note from Philip, which reached him pierced in half a dozen places and smelling vilely of sulphur and carbolic acid.

Bad news travels proverbially far and fast, and the priest of the forest learned of what had befallen Robert before his wound was whole. Early one morning he appeared at the doorway of the sick-room, and after solemnly blessing and embracing his young friend, he seated himself at the bedside and proceeded to give him all the news from his woodland home. Robert listened attentively, sometimes asking a question, again nodding an assent.

"My father," he said, suddenly breaking a pause, "tell me, if you can, who and what a certain woman by the name of Atalanta may be, or may have been, if she is dead."

"She is dead, certes, if she ever lived, which is questionable."

"Tell me all you know about her."

"It is in the nature of a fairy story," began the father, "and in such a guise you shall have it.

"Once upon a time there lived in Arcadia a beautiful maiden of the name of Atalanta. She was fleet of foot and strong of arm. The bow and arrow were her only distaff and spindle,

her hunting-dogs her dearest companions. She
lived in the woods; and you know half as well
as I myself the delights of such an existence.
She was vowed to the worship of Diana, and all
men were abhorrent to her. Nevertheless, she
had many suitors; and to rid herself of these,
she promised to wed the one of all her lovers
who could overtake and surpass the speed of
her swift white feet. She was a cruel girl and
very fair; and the luckless youths who lost in
the trial of speed were condemned to die. Many
a one lost his life; and at last, though she was
still young and lovely with the reflected beauty
of the 'orbed maiden' her mistress, there came
no more competitors for the fair prize. Then
it was that she joined the band of warriors
destined to destroy the Calydonian boar. Her
arrow first pierced the thick hide of the monster,
and at her feet Meleager, the young ruler of
Calydon, laid the spoils of the slaughtered boar.
More than this, the brave young prince offered,
kneeling before her, his heart and hand and
kingdom. But she was fiercely wedded to her
maidenhood, and would not hearken to his suit;
and when the youth lay dead, like many another
for her sake, the cold maiden kissed him, and
wept for his youth and beauty, cut short in
their green prime. But she who had overcome
so many was in her turn overcome. There

came to her at last a man with a cunning trick
which Love had taught him, who declared himself ready to run the race for which her beauty
or his life would pay the forfeit. Atalanta
was weary of strife and bloodshed, and would
have dissuaded the new-comer from the trial ;
but he taunted her with cowardice, and the tall
flower of Arcadia rose in her might and loveliness, and drawing close the girdle about her
tunic, laid aside her outer garments, and tighten-
ing her sandals about her ankles, stood ready
for the race. She looked her antagonist once
more in the face ; and as her eyes met his, she
grew afraid for the first time in all her life, —
afraid not for him, as she had been but now, but
for herself. The bold youth laughed in her face;
and red with anger she gave the signal, and the
race began. At first the man, spurred on by
love and hope, kept the lead ; but when his
breath began to fail, he heard the swift, even
footsteps of the inexorable huntress gaining on
him. She was close behind him ; the wind blew
a strand of her hair across his cheek; and at
that moment he drew from his bosom a golden
apple and threw it at her feet. He looked
behind, and saw that she had paused to pick
up the wondrous fruit, strange to her country ;
and in the time thus consumed he gained more
ground than he had lost. Again she overtook

him, rushing upon his track, the apple in her vest, her whole body strained to its utmost speed. Again the *ruse* stopped her windy way. This time the apple looked fairer still ; it grew upon a tiny branch, with bright green leaves of fairest enamelling. Yet a third time the youth was near to losing, and the goal close at hand ; one apple more remained to him, — the last gift of Venus. On this glittered dew-drops of pure clear diamonds, and on its stem bloomed forth a bunch of white blossoms, — from that day typical of bridal bliss. The girl hesitated a moment, and in the next the heralds proclaimed that she had lost the race and that the prize was won by the young stranger.

"This, as I remember it, is the old myth of Arcadian Atalanta."

"What was the name of the stranger?" demanded Robert, seizing the priest by the arm.

"Ah, my son! my memory sometimes plays me false ; his name has slipped from me. After all, what matters it ?"

"It matters a great deal, father," cried Robert, sitting up among his pillows. "Think, *think !* Is it not Milanion ?"

"Thou hast said it, my son. Where got'st thou so much knowledge ?"

For answer, Robert only hummed the refrain
of an old love-song, —

"Ai mé ! sans elle il me faut mourir."

The hot weather had come, and the city had
suddenly bloomed out with white-draped women. On the wide galleries, of an evening, one
saw groups of dark-eyed Creole girls looking like
great creamy flowers in their transparent garments of feathery white. In the streets the
heavy featured negresses on their way from market strode along with their baskets of fruit and
vegetables, clad in scant white raiment, which
made their faces blacker than ever by contrast.
In the churches the worshippers at the early
Mass looked like so many white-winged angels
kneeling at their devotions, their pinions folded
about them.

In the gardens of the Spanish fort, the West
End, the Jockey Club, white vestments glanced
through the trees and shrubbery. At nightfall
on the waters of Pontchartrain the same snowy
figures were reflected, leaning from sloop and
shallop, letting white hands trail in the cool
water. The houses too had taken on their summer dress. A deeper twilight reigned in the
high-ceiled drawing-rooms furnished in cool lin-
ens and carpeted with straw mattings. The
latticed verandas were the favorite places of

rendezvous; and Mrs. Harden, whose house stood on a breezy corner, was never obliged to complain at this season that her visitors went home too early. Darius Harden had been known unkindly to suggest that the wind-swept piazza and the matchless lemon sherbet were in some measure responsible for the difficulty with which his wife's adorers tore themselves away from her house on the hot summer evenings.

The ecstasy of iced drinks is only known by those Northerners who, like the Ruysdales, linger in New Orleans after the summer has fairly begun. The joy of the orange-flower and the pomegranate soda-water, as served by the black-eyed little Mercury at the drug-store on the corner of Rampart and Canal streets, — oh for the pen of Epicurus to write their praise in fitting phrase !

And yet that unreasonable man, General Stuart Ruysdale, was impatient to be away from New Orleans. Margaret thought it unnatural and unkind of him, and by a hundred feminine subterfuges and deceits, which six months ago she would have scorned to employ, had detained her father for several weeks after the day he had fixed for their departure. But there is an end to the patience of all men, — and the end, be it said, is usually very near to the beginning. The time came when General Ruysdale put his military foot down and ordered that all should be made ready for the retreat northward.

The Atalanta was finished ; the store of slippers and shoes from the matchless shoemaker of Royal Street had come home ; the races at the Fair Grounds had been won and lost ; and the great sham battle between the veterans and the younger militiamen, and the famous competitive drill, were things of the past. The day of departure had been set, and the General, not without some feeling of regret, was taking leave of his new-made friends, first among whom was his old-time adversary, Colonel Lagrange. The Colonel had agreed to visit the Ruysdales at their New England home during the summer, and the General had hesitated about renewing his lease of the little house where they had passed so happy a winter. The hesitation was, however, only momentary. When he remembered the fears that had at times beset him of ever getting his daughter safely away from that city of fascinating men, he said to himself with a half sigh : " No, never again ; the risk is too great." For the General was nothing but a poor, foolish old man after all, as we shall see ; and the quiet Margaret, the girl whose whole life had been devoted to him and to the art that was their mutual delight, had undergone a change as wonderful and yet as natural as had been the

sudden breaking of the winter into the splendor
of the Southern spring.

She was sitting in her studio late one afternoon, talking with Sara Harden, who had come
to see the bas-relief for the last time, when a
card was brought to Miss Ruysdale. Her visitor
saw the flush that spread over her face as Margaret read the name and asked that the caller
should be shown into the studio.

" As I was saying when I was interrupted,"
Mrs. Harden went on, " I think your bas-relief a
great success, barring the figure of the Milanion,
which I never did like. The huntsmen, the
group of girls, the dogs in the leash, are most
natural. The Atalanta I like best, of course, because it is your little graceful self, — though why
you ever put yourself in such a character I can't
imagine. You now could never be won by such
a *ruse,* — rousing your curiosity or cupidity by
throwing a golden apple in your path. Fancy
it ! "

" Oh, but it means so much more than that,"
said Margaret. " Atalanta really wanted to be
won, you know, only she was ashamed to say so,
after all, — all her protestations to the contrary ;
and Milanion had seen that in her face."

" What liberties you take with the myths, my
dear ! Don't judge the Arcadian Atalanta by
yourself, I beg of you. And yet, I don't know, —

she married the winner in the race, though a better and a braver man was dead for her sake. She was like many another woman before and since her time. One wonders a little if she ever realized in after days that Meleager was a prince among men, and that the gold of his true heart was less mixed with dross than the gold of the apple of Hesperides. She had both in her hands. Did she ever dream in the still night-watches that she had thrown away the gold and kept the dross ? *Qui sait ?* Here comes your visitor, — Milanion himself, upon my word ! I must take my own leave, as no one seems to care to take leave of me."

Robert Feuardent had entered the studio, and stood looking at Margaret with eyes that could see nothing but her. Without noticing her friend, who had slipped from the room, Margaret came to meet her guest with a few stereotyped words of welcome on her lips.

" Mr. Feuardent, I am so glad to see you so well — so much better. It 's a long time since we have met, is it not ? "

" A lifetime, Atalanta."

She was trembling all over, and her hands had grown suddenly perfectly cold. Robert, in whose mind there could not fail to be a memory of that morning when he had last entered the studio, full of health and hope and love, only to leave it wounded and senseless, was very grave. He was still weak, and the emotion which the sight of Margaret had roused, together with these painful recollections, gave him a sudden moment of faintness. She placed a chair for him, and by the time she had in a measure controlled the nervous trembling which had come over her, he was himself again.

"The Count tells me you are thinking of leaving soon," he began.

" Yes," said Margaret, looking bravely in his face, with a laugh which had little of merriment, " yes, we must go next week, papa says. You know it is late in the season for us Northerners to linger here, and the fever is at Thebes, — that makes him anxious, naturally."

" Of course," said Robert severely, "quite right, I am sure ; it makes me anxious myself." Then, noticing Margaret's look of astonishment, he added : " Not for myself, of course ; I have had the fever already, as you know, — but for you."

" It 's very good of you."

" Whât is good of me ? "

" To be anxious about me."

" How can I help it ? " this with a look which was a love-poem in itself.

" You must take your last look at Atalanta to-day," said Margaret, ignoring the poem, " she is to be boxed to-morrow. She is going to be

exhibited, poor thing, in New York. Are n't you
sorry for her and for me ?   We shall both be so
dreadfully criticised.   You cannot conceive the
sort of terror that grows upon me when I have
nearly finished a piece of work, — the fear of ridicule.   I don't mind being told that I don't know
anything about art, that my modelling is bad,
my conception weak, my execution anything but
what it should be; but I do mind being laughed
at, for my work, faulty as it is, has been done in
very serious earnest, and it seems but fair that
if it is to be condemned, it should be in a spirit
of serious criticism, not of flippant satire."

" I should like to know who would dare to treat
you or your work with disrespect.   I — I would
kill any man who dared to speak of it as you say."
He looked fierce enough to carry out his threat.

Margaret laughed, saying : " And the women,
what would you do to them ?   They are unap-
proachable, and under the invulnerable armor of
their sex they discharge the poisoned arrows of
envy, slander, and all uncharitableness ; and we,
the workers, must endure it without a 'murmur,
for they, being but talkers, can always have the
last word."

" Are they all like this ? "

" No, good friend ; thank Heaven, there are
very few such traitors in the army of working
women."

Robert moved uneasily in his chair, and said after a pause : " Do not talk to me about your work; it makes you so unlike the *you* I know best."

· " And that is — ? "

" That is the girl who danced with me at the *fête*, who gathered roses with me an hour after sunrise, the sister of charity who brought me soup while I was ill, and whose image has haunted my sick-room ever since she — "

Margaret interrupted him.

" It is the same I — always — " She stooped and straightened the rug upon the floor, and then took a seat a little farther away from the man whose eyes glowed with so strange a light. It made her tremble again, and the trouble in her seemed all centred in her heart, for she laid her hand upon her breast as if to stay its beating ; and Robert saw the action, and knew what it meant far better than she could have told him, for love was to him not so new a thing as to this Northern maiden, in whose veins flowed the pure cool blood of the Puritans. Because it is not an easy thing for these women to let Love into their hearts, so is it impossible for them ever to drive him out ; for the overthrow must be absolute and irrevocable before the sweet surrender is made. Something of this the man felt ; and with the feeling came an awe of the girl whose white

impassioned face was turned to him, and a resolve that the love he read so plainly in her
eyes should be held as the most sacred thing
in his life, which should henceforth be kept
clean and pure, a fitting temple to enshrine so
white a flame.

"And you are going to leave me, Atalanta?"

"Yes."

"May I come after you?" — she smiled, —
"and bring you back with me," — she blushed
deliciously and cast down her eyes, — "to stay
forever?"

He was close beside her now, and stood with
outstretched arms looking at her with an expression which sent the terrified blood back in a flood
upon her heart.

"Come!" he murmured.

She sprang to her feet with an instinct of
flight, and glided from him toward the door.
The sudden motion jarred the room, and from
the wall an orange dropped from the branch she
had hung there weeks ago. It rolled towards
Margaret and under her fleet feet, which tripped
on the treacherous fruit. She stumbled, and
would have fallen, but that a pair of arms was
ready to uphold her. A little cry, half of fright,
half of love, escaped her pale lips as she felt
herself folded to a heart beating quite as fast
as her own. She struggled to be free for one

moment longer; and then, remembering that he was still weak from his wound, she gave a low sigh and lay still for one glad moment in his arms.

And so the golden apple was responsible for all the trouble and all the joy that followed, as it was in the days of Eve and in the time of Arcadian Atalanta.

It did not prove a difficult matter for Robert to tell Margaret that he loved her, and to convince her that he must have her for his own. The arguments he used need not be set down here; they were somewhat indistinctly uttered, and yet were thoroughly understood. They were not new arguments, but have been frequently employed before, — usually with success, as every reader ought to know. For life is but a poor treadmill existence after all, a sort of dry-crust we all have to eat, and love may be prosaically compared to a kind of golden butter which transforms the hard morsel to the ambrosia of the Gods. It is a cheap luxury, the poorest may have it; and yet how many *soi-disant* world philosophers to-day go fasting, on the plea that it is too costly a thing to feed upon!

Robert found it a very easy thing to convince Margaret, as we have said, but it was a very different matter when it came to convincing Margaret's father, of the soundness of his argu-

ments. They were not indeed even listened
to ; for when poor Robert had got as far in his
story as to tell the General that he loved his
only daughter and wanted her for his wife, he
was spared the trouble of going any farther.
Stuart Ruysdale thanked him for the honor he
had done him in asking his daughter's hand,
but absolutely declined to bestow it upon him.
Robert, who an hour before had assured Margaret that it would be a positive injury to his
health to postpone their marriage for more than
a month, said falteringly that he could wait any
length of time, — a year, two, three, ay, ten
years, — a lifetime, even, if he were only allowed
to hope. But even hope was denied him ; he
was told that her father had other views for
Margaret. "Was there a preferred lover?" he
demanded fiercely, with an inward resolution to
have his life if such a one existed. No, there
was no other suitor ; Miss Ruysdale had never
been a figure in the matrimonial market. She
was devoted to things less trivial and unsatisfactory ; she was, in point of fact, too much
absorbed in her art to think of marriage at
present.

"At present!" cried Robert aghast; "when
then shall she think of it ? When she is *wold* ?"
There were some sounds in the English language which he never had been able to master,

for he had not learned to speak it until he was sixteen years of age.

The General looked annoyed at this remark.

"Miss Ruysdale is still quite young enough to wish to devote the next few years of her life to the art in which she has already given such undoubted marks of ability. This interview is very painful to me, Mr. Feuardent; I must beg you to let it draw to a close. I will repeat, in parting with you, that there is nothing at all derogatory to you in my refusal of your suit."

In a desperate note, full of love and grief and despair, Robert communicated the result of the interview to Margaret.

The General ate his dinner alone that night, Margaret pleading a severe headache as her excuse for not appearing. This put the old soldier in a still less amiable frame of mind; and when he had finished his solitary meal, he lit his cigar and took his way toward the club,—that retreat of all erring men when in disgrace at home.

Here he found Colonel Lagrange, and the two worthies settled down to a game of chess; but before they had been seated a half hour in the Egyptian passivity of that unnatural and awful game, the General declared himself entirely incapable of fixing his mind upon his men. He needed a confidant; and retiring to one of the quiet recesses of the card-room, he told his friend what had passed between himself and Feuardent that afternoon.

"Do you think your daughter is interested in the young man ?" the Colonel inquired.

"*Interested* is too strong a term. I think she fancies the fellow a little, especially since his accident," the father reluctantly admitted.

"If *you* think that she fancies him, that is enough to convince me that she is in love with him."

"How can she tell? She does n't know anything about love ; she is not like other girls, Colonel. And you know as well as I do the worth of these first attachments, — mere flashes in the pan."

"I know what they are worth a great deal better than you do, or than you pretend to. If Miss Margaret was my daughter, I should be very thankful to bestow her hand on the first man who had touched her heart. It's a dangerous thing, sir, when a woman learns that though love is eternal, its object may be very variable. You and I know that ; but God forbid that our daughters should learn the fact. Depend upon it, the girl who marries the first man she falls in love with makes the most faithful and satisfied wife. She looks upon it as a definite thing ; she is born once, loves and marries

once, and dies once; and that's an end of it.
Now, your girl who is in love half-a-dozen times
before her marriage has learned so much of
the mutability of things, of men in especial, that
she is pretty safe to repeat the sensation after
matrimony."

"Other things being equal, I admit there is
some truth in what you say; but in this case
look at the immense disadvantages," the General
demurred. "Is Feuardent in a position to marry
my daughter? Is he disinterestedly attached to
her? Though in our part of the world I am
not a rich man, nor my daughter an heiress,
here, where the scale is so different, her fortune
may be an important item in the young man's
calculations."

"There you wrong Robert, there you wrong
our society, General Ruysdale. Thank God, sir!
we have not yet arrived, in this community, at
that stage of social development — decomposi-
tion, I call it — where marriages of reason are
made. No, sir, my young friend is able to marry
for love; and if you disinherited your daughter
to-morrow, he would ask you again for her
hand."

The Colonel buttoned up his coat to the very
chin, as was his habit in moments of excitement,
and rubbed imaginary dust from the sleeve of
his well-brushed, threadbare coat.

"I may have done the young man an injustice," said the General, endeavoring to mollify his friend. "Admitting that his regard is as pure as you claim it to be, the great differences of education, of character, of tastes, of race, and of religion, are they not incompatible with a happy marriage?"

"No, sir; I don't care a button for those bugbears. Love is too strong for any and all of them combined; he can knock 'em out in the first round. It would be a good thing if there were more marriages of this sort, General. You New England folks go on marrying and intermarrying with each till your asylums are full of insane people from the eternal consanguinity of your alliances. Your natures grow colder and more intellectual in each generation; while here in the South we are still too much under the sway of our emotions, and a little of the chilly intellectuality of the Northern race would be a good leaven. If I were President of these United States I should legislate to the end of amalgamating the too-cold Northern and the over-hot Southern blood. In two generations we should have the finest race of people, sir, that has existed in this world since the day when Adam broke his alliance with the brutes and called himself man, and their master."

The Colonel had warmed up to his theme,

20

and was pacing up and down the small alcove, gesticulating to his audience, — the one-armed General.

"Very good generalities," grumbled the latter; "but for all your theories, I don't propose to give my daughter to the first black-eyed penniless Creole who fancies her, to illustrate them."

"And why not, sir? Ah! I smell your money-bags behind all that. It hurts you to think that your money may be spent, wasted even, or lost in the South. Now, look at the stupidity of the situation. Here is the North, so rich that money is a drug in the market. You can't invest it to bring you more than four per cent; and rather than risk it at that, your rich men literally sit down on their money-bags, instead of letting the money go out to earn more. Here is the South, the undeveloped country, the richest land in the world, where the earth's crust yields its harvest with less pain to man than in any other quarter of the globe, where the earth's bowels are lined with ores and gems and precious minerals, — all this treasure is waiting to enrich the whole land; and yet it remains locked in the earth, waiting till the key, capital, shall be fitted to the lock. It's positively insane! And what's the consequence? New York, that den of robber-barons, keeps the bulk of the wealth of the country as a species of giant playthings for

the half-dozen cleverest rogues to play a game
of skittles with, bowling down every man who
tries to stand up against their infernal tricks.
Why, the vast fortunes thus accumulated, which
have wrought such malign effects on the country,
never could have been possible if the people of the
North had used their brains and put their money
into developing the country, in some degree, to
an equal prosperity. It 's a devil's game they
play, those dozen or two so-called 'money-kings,'
and it is your own fault that you are tumbled
down, like so many tenpins, by their heavy balls.
The result is ruinous all the way down to your
lowest classes. The greatest gambling-hell the
world has ever seen has for its croupiers these
great men, whose names you mention with bated
breath. 'Financiers,' you call them ; swindlers
and gamblers they should be termed. All over
the land bank-presidents, trustees, men in the
highest offices of State and private trust, are
tempted to their ruin and the ruin of their
dependents through the accursed influence of
these men, who have set up the golden calf
in our midst and cast down the gods of our
forefathers."·

Though Margaret did not appear at dinner
that evening, her headache did not prevent her
from slipping out to see Sara Harden the moment
the General departed for his club. She found

her faithful friend cold and indifferent; and when she finally knelt beside her, and putting her arms about her waist told her the whole story and begged for help and sympathy, the unaccountable little woman said nothing, but began to cry bitterly. Margaret rose to her feet silent and hurt. Why did every one turn against her when she so needed sympathy in her new-found happiness? She was learning that it is more rare to find natures that can rejoice with us in our joys than those that are willing to mourn with us in our griefs. No one envies our misfortunes or disgrace; but there are few who can look with perfect equanimity on our success or happiness. Blessed are they that mourn; but more blessed are they that can unfeignedly rejoice in the joy of their brother.

At last Mrs. Harden dried her blue eyes; and taking Margaret in her arms, kissed her and wished her all happiness.

"I had to cry a little, dear, for my heart was set on a very different lover for you; and you know that he is now in that pest-stricken city, working like an angel among the sick and dying. You must not grudge him my few tears."

It was Margaret's turn to cry now, and they took what comfort they could out of their tears, as women will; and then, when their eyes were quite dry, they looked the situation in the face

and talked over their plan of action. For not-
withstanding her loyalty to Philip, Mrs. Harden
was too thoroughly feminine a woman not to
take delight in helping a love affair along over
the proverbially rough course.

" I will see the General myself," Mrs. Harden
finally said, after they had discussed the very
simple matter at the greatest length, looking at
it from all possible, probable, and impossible
points of view. "Of course he will give in;
there's nothing else for him to do. You won't
give Robert up ? No ? Quite sure ? "

" Never !" said Margaret solemnly.

" And the young man himself, will he be
equally steadfast ? "

" Can you doubt him ? "

"Of course I can, my dear, because I always
doubt everybody, — lovers in especial ; but the
question is, can *you* doubt him ? "

" I could more easily doubt myself."

" You are deliciously in love, Margaret, and
I will try to forgive you for loving. the wrong
man ; though *how* you could — well, no matter !
Don't be angry ; leave your papa to Darius and
me, we will fix him between us."

" *Mr.* Harden — why, *why* Mr. Harden, what
good can he do ? "

" A man 's a great support in times like these,
Margaret, they really are. They put the other

man at such a disadvantage, — if you understand what I mean by that sort of thing. Your father, now, could appeal to my sympathies as well as I to his ; but Darius, — I put it to you, who would think of appealing to Darius's sympathy ? He won't have any; he's Robert's friend; he can bear testimony to his character, his family, his property, and his political sentiments. Oh, Darius will have to come too ; I could n't think of facing the implacable father without my old Gaffer Harden to back me."

" Well, dear, you know best; but — "

" Of course I do ; but me no buts. A husband is so convenient in a row ; I call Dari my fighting editor. But to return to the General. Under the combined attack of fatherly affection and remorse, of Sara and Darius Harden, of Robert and Margaret, with the support of Colonel Lagrange thrown in if necessary, the rout will be complete."

And it was.

The enemy held out valiantly for a week, and then, after an heroic resistance, was routed, — horse, foot, and dragoon breaking under the final charge of the foe, which was the more deadly because of the heavy shower of tears under which it was made. Peace was restored, and the articles signed on terms which were creditable to both parties. The General was to retire to his

Northern home, taking his prisoner, Margaret, with him, while her heart was left as hostage in the hands of that disturber of the peace, Robert Feuardent, who gave bonds to appear when the summer was over and restore the hostage, only again to take possession of it and the prisoner in the early autumn days, when the land should be glad with the fulness of the harvest.

And so with heavy hearts Margaret and Robert parted, each full of gloomy forebodings that they should not live to see that golden day when the virgin Atalanta should turn from the worship of Diana to burn incense before the altar of Hymen.

Ah, me! for those fond, foolish, loving days whose pain seems unendurable, those partings and meetings which tear the heart-strings, how quickly do they pass! How tenderly are they remembered in the after-time, when love has cooled, even if it has strengthened into steadfast affection. We agonize over the love-tortures, and cry out that they make life too hard for us to bear; and yet when they are past and gone, we count each moment of that time as a grain of gold in the sombre sands of life, and would gladly give a year of the prosaic contentment of our prosperous lives for one moment of that pain which is the most pleasureful thing that life has held for us!

CHAPTER XIX.

THERESE CASENEUVE, Philip Rondelet, and the faithful Hero were made welcome at Thebes. The greeting that awaited them was a solemn one. People looked them in the face searchingly ; and reading there the look that they sought, took them by the hand and bade them welcome to the city of death. The band of workers, the doctors, the nurses, and the men of God already come together from all parts of the Union,— North, South, East, and West, — recognized in the new-comers three strong helpers fit to undertake the labor of which only the noblest men and women are capable. The outgoing trains, that stopped a mile from the city, daily bore away people fleeing from the pestilence, deserting friend and loved one in a mad panic of fear which overcame every better feeling ; but the incoming trains brought men and women, even youths and girls, who came to labor amidst strangers, — a labor whose only earthly reward might be death in its most terrible form, a hasty and unsanctified burial, and a nameless grave in the potter's field. For the pestilence that walketh by night had smitten the fair town of Thebes as pray God city may never again be visited in this land of ours ! What sin was there in the town that it should be thus chastened with a punishment more awful than that which befell Sodom and Gomorrah ? They were wiped out all in one hour, and after a brief agony their sinners slept at peace ; in Thebes each hour saw a new agony, each day a fresh list of victims.

What law had its citizens broken that they were so afflicted? Alas ! the law which commands that cleanliness should be held as only second to godliness, — that commandment which, if it be set at nought, brings so terrible a punishment to the offenders.

Philip, wishing to keep Therese as much under his care as possible, suggested that some one of the many houses which the richer folk had deserted should be turned into a hospital where the homeless sick, those creatures who were daily stricken down in the streets and public places, might be brought and tended. No sooner had he made this plan known than he was informed that one of the largest houses in the town was at his disposal. Its owner herself sought him out, and begged that without delay he would take possession of her dwelling. She

was a striking-looking woman, about forty years
of age, showing traces of a remarkable beauty.
Her soft brown eyes and gentle, magnetic voice
attracted him strongly, as with simple generosity
she gave him possession of her house and all
that it contained, only reserving to herself the
right, to share in nursing the patients.   That
very day saw her richly furnished dwelling transformed into a pest-house, where the nameless
sufferers of the streets were tended with the
greatest care and devotion.   Madame Anna —
for so this woman was called — never spared
herself, and day and night was found at her
post, faithful and self-contained.   The dreadful
sights, the heart-rending scenes, before which
Therese often grew sick and faint, and which
it took all Philip's strength to endure, Madame
Anna bore with a composure and fortitude which
gave her fellow-workers fresh courage.   Madame
Anna, a woman of the town, whose sumptuous
house had seen such unholy orgies, now passed
from room to room, ministering to the wretched
sufferers, the off-scouring of the streets, the very
lowest of whom in other days had claimed the
right to scoff at her.   To this strangely assorted
band of workers came one more, Virginia Allen,
a girl from a New England town, as fair and
good and young as Margaret herself.   She had
come to join the noble army of martyrs ; and

Philip, finding that she was wretchedly housed, prayed Madame Anna's hospitality for her — for Margaret's sake, to whom he fancied she bore a far-away resemblance.

Money and clothing, stores and medicine, were sent them daily from Northern cities, in which the pitiful cry for help was generously answered ; and the people flocked to the house of the Magdalen to receive the goods and rations daily dealt out to them.

Famine was upon the city, though the fields were white with cotton, and the city full of laborers, able-bodied, but incapacitated by terror for work ; and the burden of these hungry idlers seemed sometimes too heavy to be endured.

Summer was over all the land ; the trees had leafed, and the flowers bloomed with a beauty and fulness which, by contrast to the squalor and horror of the city, seemed unprecedented. The weather was halcyon, the skies cloudless, the air — save where it blew over some tainted quarter — sweet and languorous. At mid-day the sun burned fiercely in the heavens ; but at night the moonlight turned the city into a fairy-land. Snatching a brief hour of repose after a day of ceaseless toil, Philip sat upon the gallery looking out upon the garden, where all was quiet. The street was deserted ; not a sound broke the magic stillness. The full moon blazed in midheaven with a radiance such as he had never before seen. Peace seemed spread abroad; the shrieks of delirium, the labored breath and strangling groan of the death agony were stilled. For a moment all the terrible reality by which he was surrounded was forgotten, and Philip sat dreaming of the cool sea-girt city from which he had that day received tidings of Margaret. She had sent a contribution of money and of clothing. He had recognized among the many useful articles of dress a pair of tiny satin shoes, half-worn, and holding still the impress of her foot. They were modish little shoes, high-instepped and silver-buckled, inappropriate enough for the class of women for whom they were sent; but they seemed to Philip Rondelet like a talisman, and he had kissed them and put them in his breast, as if they had been sent him for a love-token. Some one touched him on the shoulder, calling him back from that blessed moment of oblivion to the fearful intensity of the present; it was Virginia. He started to his feet, feeling as guilty as a drowsing picket challenged on his post.

"What is it, my child?"

"The priest I watched with last night died this morning; there is not one other clergyman who is not down with the fever. They have come to take him. Can we not go to see him buried? It seems too terrible, after all that he has done, that there should be no word said over him, no friend to follow him to his grave."

Philip hesitated. His charge was with the living, his time and strength were too precious to waste with the dead ; but the girl went on and would not be denied.

"Come, let us go, the drive will do us both good ; I have not been in the air for nearly a week. You must come with me, or I will call Therese and we will go alone."

"Therese is asleep, and Madame Anna begged that we should not wake her ; she has not been in bed for many nights. I will go with you, Virginia, but we must hasten ; I have still to make my rounds to-night."

All barriers of caste were swept away in this terrible time. Anna the Magdalen, Virginia the pure, delicate Northern maiden, Therese the hunted fugitive flying from the law, Rondelet the fastidious aristocrat and man of the world, addressed each other by their Christian names, as if they had been brother and sisters to one another in blood, as they were in their self-abnegation and faith.

A rude cart stood waiting ; they took their seats as best they might beside the rough pine coffin, and with Hero and one other negro for guides, made their way to the city of the dead, to which came each day more and more denizens. The wide gates stood hospitably open, — there was little need to close them now; and under the shadow of the white cross reared high over the entrance the funeral *cortège* moved rapidly to its destination. No time in these days for solemn march or death-dirge, the sick claimed all the time of those that were whole; none might linger with the dead.

They reached the grave, and Virginia slipped into Philip's hand the prayer-book open at the burial-service. By the light of the moon, with the two bearers and Virginia kneeling beside him, Philip read aloud the sentences of that great service of the Church of England, — the most glorious and immortal jewel that our language enshrines. When he had said the last words, a sweet, trembling voice which grew stronger at every measure was lifted up, and Virginia sang a hymn of hope and of triumph. The men had already begun the task of filling the grave, but high above the dull sound of the clotted earth striking upon the coffin-lid rose the joyous chant which the virgin martyr sang over the priest whose footsteps she was soon to follow to the land beyond the grave.

In the weeks which followed, Philip Rondelet saw men and women tried, as it is not often given to man to be tried, in a fiery furnace of suffering and pain. All that is best, all that is worst, in humanity was brought out under the crucial test. People who might in other times have lived and died unconscious of the heroism latent in their souls figured as martyrs in the doomed community, while others who had stood high in public esteem, as in their own eyes, were branded with the shameful epithets of coward and traitor. Husbands deserted wives, and fathers children ; but the records failed to show one case of a woman who betrayed the trust of husband, parent, or child. And this testimony, given by a man who passed through the terrible epidemic at Thebes, it is gratifying for a woman here to set down. In this life-and-death struggle, as in that other time of battle, the blacks were faithful to their trust ; and though most of the great houses and much valuable property were left entirely in their hands, there is not one instance where the master, flying from the pestilence and leaving his goods in the hands of his servant, found just cause for complaint on his return.

The days went by, and the summer drew to its close. In a few weeks the coming of the cold weather would check the plague; but in these weeks the fever raged at its very worst, as if eager to grasp more and always more victims before the spirit of the frost should exorcise it and the broken people be at peace. The ranks of workers grew thinner and thinner, and those that were spared strained their utmost strength to do the work that was laid upon them. The days of weeping were long past. The strong grew cheerful, each one in his endeavor to keep up the courage of his fellows. The weak became reckless, and it was not an unusual thing, in that reign of terror, to hear harsh laughter and grim bravado and jest as one passed through the desolate streets. This phase was perhaps the most terrible one that Philip encountered. He found one day a drunken, blaspheming husband beside a dying wife, and in the next room a mother singing to a writhing child, soothing and petting the little one she still hoped to save, while they were bearing away from her the other darling she had watched and prayed over in vain.

It was at this time, in the fiercest stress and terror, that Virginia Allen passed on to the reward that awaited her. The two women and the man beside whom she had worked so faithfully nursed her with a care which would have saved her, had it not been written that she should die in the midst of her toil. She died, this fair Northern girl, having given her life to succor the sick and dying of a stranger city. O South! can there be any bitterness left in your hearts against a North which has laid so

white a sacrifice before the awful demon of the
pestilence that laid your fairest cities desolate ?
One such pure life — and there were many such
given — should efface the memory of a Gettys-
burg and a Shiloh.

A great grief fell upon those that were left
when the youngest and frailest of them was
taken. Now that they had lost her, it seemed
to them that Virginia had been the strongest of
the four ; and Madame Anna, who till then had
never lost her quiet cheerfulness, never smiled
again. Each one asked himself or herself :
"Which one of us next ? " Philip had succeeded
so wonderfully with his patients, turning out
more convalescents than any other doctor, that
they had all felt perfect faith in him and in his
ability to save them and himself. From the outside world, which stood aghast at the tales of
suffering and death which every day's bulletin
told, came help, and, what was better, sympathy.
It is not probable that those who penned the
words of praise and of sympathy that found their
way through mail and press and telegraph to
the devoted city ever realized what cordial to the
fainting souls these loving messages proved.
Robert and Margaret, Sara Harden and many
another loyal friend, in this way helped to keep
up Philip's courage and strength, on which the
great draughts drawn daily were beginning to

tell. His fine nervous constitution was tasked to its fullest capacity ; and now the reserve force — that last fund of human endurance — was coming into play. He had grown thinner and paler, and his eyes looked larger and more unfathomably deep than ever. Those blue-gray eyes, which had burned with so tender a light of love for Margaret Ruysdale, now seemed gifted with a power of seeing beyond the vision of other men, and tender with a love surpassing that of a lover for his mistress.

Therese had grown stronger and better, in spite of the hard labor which was so new to her. The cankering bitterness which had eaten her heart was all gone now ; in the awful reality in which she lived, things before and behind her shone out in their true colors. She saw and repented her own sin, and was glad of the expiation in which she believed she was atoning for her past. Her greatest anxiety was centred in Philip, whom she watched and guarded with a jealous care, sparing his strength and foreseeing his every wish, in her desire to save him all unnecessary fatigue. She had grown wonderfully gentle and tender, the poor half-crazed Therese, and Hero himself was not more humble and faithful in ministering to his master than was she. She had never greatly feared the fever for herself ; it was for Philip that she grew more and more anxious as the weeks went by, each one taking with it a little and a little more of his strength. At last she spoke to him, and begged him to begone while there was yet time.

They were watching beside Madame Anna, who had at last been overtaken by the fever, and whose vigorous physique was struggling with the destroyer, when Therese suddenly laid her hand on Philip's arm and entreated him to leave Thebes.

"And leave you, Therese? No, my child, we are now seeing the beginning of the end ; for the last three days the new cases have been diminishing, and the character of the disease has become less malignant. More recover than die now."

"Yes, and for that reason you must go. You have done your work ; the worst is past. I will stay with Madame Anna till she is well, or till all is over. There is no danger for me ; it rarely attacks my people."

Since she had learned that her blood was tainted by that inferior strain, which until it is removed to the thirty-second degree, according to the old *code noir*, outbalances the purer blood and makes the individual a person of color, Therese had always spoken of herself as belonging to the African race. And yet Therese Case-

neuve, half sister of Robert Feuardent, bore no
vestige of African descent, unless it was in the
deep notes of her voice, pathetic and passionate
in turn, or in her almost savage health and its
attendant perfection of form.   That one burning
drop of negro blood had blighted her life; the
knowledge of it had transformed the man who
was her plighted husband into her destroyer.   It
had brought shame and sin and death to him;
it had changed her from a happy, hopeful girl
into a desperate and sinful woman, conscience-
stricken and wellnigh a fratricide.

Madame Anna grew worse.   It was evident
that the fever had overcome her stout resistance.
She herself saw that hope was past; and desir-
ing to set her affairs in order, she summoned to
her bedside her man of business, a mulatto who
had been faithful to her even as were her new-
made friends.

When she had talked long and earnestly with
him she slept for a space, and then begged that
she might be left alone with Therese.   The interview was a long one, and lasted far into the night.
Philip never knew what was said between the
two erring women, — the one standing at the
end of a career the saddest that falls to human
lot, tarnished by a thousand sins, weighed down
with the sense of the infinite woe and disgrace
her life had brought upon other lives; the other

trembling, affrighted, perhaps on the verge of such an existence, with the knowledge of evil in her eyes and the shrinking from sin haply not yet overcome in her heart. What future was there for this poor Therese, full of good and evil impulses, born of a race of slaves, bred with the tastes and ambitions of a refined gentlewoman, in whose veins surged the evil passions to which she owed her birth, in whose soul burned an inextinguishable hunger for a higher life?

When at last Philip came into Madame Anna's chamber, he found the Magdalen lying peacefully at rest, with Therese sleeping in the chair beside her from sheer exhaustion. The girl's eyes were swollen with weeping, and her slumber was broken by frequent sighs. The patient's face wore a calm look; and when he touched her hand, Philip knew that her sleep would know no waking.

In the days that followed, Philip learned that Madame Anna's house and land and all her other property had been willed to Therese for her sole use and pleasure. He never learned of the condition on which this rich legacy was given, nor of the solemn vow to observe it that Therese had made, with no other witness than the dying woman. The money that had been so miserably earned was to be expended, not in requiem masses for the dead, but in a manner far more likely to absolve the soul of the Magdalen from its punishment, — if it be true, as Therese believed, that the heartfelt prayers of the living can speed the dead on their journey toward eternal peace.

CHAPTER XX.

GOLDEN September has come and gone, and brown October, her elder sister, more sober and not less beautiful than the yellow month, is here. The nuts are ripe, the corn is gathered, the apples stand in high pyramids in the four corners of the orchards, — one pile russet-brown, one rosy red, another deep yellow, and the fourth green with the color of the famous greening, the best apple in the world for cider and tart. It is the merry season of the year in good New England. The farmer's lads and lasses, who have not stolen one day's holiday during the busy time of ploughing the soil and planting the seed, of tending the ripening crops and finally of harvesting the fruits of the earth, now take what little of rest and pleasure the year holds for them. The county Agricultural Fair has drawn people together from the remote hamlets and scattered farms which radiate from the centre of Woodbridge. The roads are alive with vehicles of all degrees, from the ox-cart laden with giant vegetables on its way to the Fair, to the spider

of the farmer jockey, bound to try the speed of
the colt he has raised against that of the other
contestants in the race. Here come a pair of
rustic lovers in a trim farm-wagon newly var-
nished for the occasion. They have a stout
plough-horse, whose speed the unwary youth
pits against that of the slender steed of a city
shopman who, with a horse and chaise hired for
the occasion, is bringing the lady of his choice
out to the Fair. The city horse is a nervous,
light-limbed creature, which at a touch of the
whip springs forward into a swift gait, his fleet
hoofs tossing the·dust into the face of the dis-
comfited farmer, who is soon left far behind. In
the hour of defeat it is little comfort for him to
reflect that had the race-course been a field, the
vehicle a harrow, the results would have been
very different. .

From her favorite seat, high up in the arms of
a giant apple-tree, Margaret watches the line of
wagons and wayfarers passing down the high-
road that bounds the orchard. She looks with
careless interest at the farmers and their wives,
at the townspeople and the gentlefolk, as they
pass on their way to the Fair, her eyes always
reverting to a point in the road where the first
glimpse of a carriage returning from the station
may be had. At last! There are the grays,
behind them her father, a fearless driver, and at

his side the man whose coming she has so long anticipated. Once sure that he is there, her interest in the carriage ceases ; she buries her face in her hands, and for an instant contemplates mounting to a still loftier aerie at the very top of the great tree. The idea is dismissed as being childish : the old orchard always makes her feel herself a child again ; and descending lightly from the tree, she stands beneath its shadow, afraid to go back to the house to meet him, and dreading lest he should fail to find her in the orchard. She hears a step on the path, a shadow falls across the heap of red-gold pumpkins on the other side of the wall, the gate swings open and shuts again, and some one stands beside her. She does not look up ; she dares not lift her eyes to his face, lest she should find it changed.

" Won't you speak to me, Margaret ? "

She is silent.

" Look at me, at least ; I have come so far."

He is devouring her with his eyes, which find her bonnier than ever ; but still she cannot look at him. It is as if her eyelids were weighed down with the burden of the happy tears which sparkle from under the long lashes.

" Atalanta, are you not glad that I have come to you ? Shall I go ? "

There is a shade of reproach in his voice. With an effort of will she lifts her eyes slowly

till they rest on his collar, and then pause as if
intent on studying the jewel in his scarf. He
steps back a pace, as if to go ; then the eyes
flash upward into his, the glad color pulses to
her cheek and brow, for at what she sees all her
fear is forgotten.

Never did days fly by as did those that followed Robert's arrival at Woodbridge.   There
was so much for him to see, there were so many
people for him to meet, that every hour was
filled.   He had never been at the North, and
everything he saw had the interest of novelty.
The beautiful old Ruysdale house, which was new
when the century was young, with its treasures
of ancient carving, of ancestral silver, its family
portraits by Stuart and Copley, its miniatures
by Malbone of the dead-and-gone Ruysdales, all
sleeping in the graveyard of the old church
which the founder of the family had erected.
Then there were the living Ruysdales, even more
awesome to Feuardent's mind, — the General's
aunt and Margaret's several dozens of cousins,
all of whom felt themselves privileged to mystify
and embarrass him as to their puzzling names
and identity.   Margaret was immensely popular
in this large family circle, and not a day passed in
which Robert was not made to understand what a
lucky fellow he was, — first in winning a Ruysdale
for his wife, and secondly in that the particular

Ruysdale he had won was the sweet maid Margaret. The Ruysdales were a powerful clan, and a proud one. They had some right to be so. They had furnished a governor to the Colony in the old days, and ever since that time members of the family had held offices of trust in the State and had stood high in public esteem. All this Robert was made to appreciate fully by the afore-mentioned relatives, " who rubbed it in extra hard," Mrs. Harden observed to her husband, " because they did n't know when they should catch a real live Creole fresh from Louisiana again."

The Hardens had come to share in Margaret's happiness, and Colonel Lagrange with Bouton de Rose, who was to stand by Robert in the hour of need as best man, was hourly expected. The wedding-day had been set, and the mail and express-carriers were bringing boxes and packages every day, whose contents were of the most profound interest to all the female cousins, as well as to Sara Harden and Margaret herself. One afternoon, about a fortnight before the happy day, Margaret and Robert, returning from one of their long rambles through the crispy autumn woods, encountered Mrs. Harden strolling leisurely along, leaning on the arm of a young and good-looking Ruysdale of the other sex.

" I was looking for you, young moon-doves,"
she began, " because I want to separate you for
one brief half hour. I have something very particular to say to my dear Margaret. Gentlemen,
we will excuse you."

Margaret knew what was coming, and looked
down uneasily, rolling a ribbon end between her
fingers.

" Dear, I wanted to ask you if you had written
to Philip when it is to be ? "

" No, Sara."

" I think you ought."

" He will have heard, don't you think so ? "

" How can one tell ? — he is so shut off from
the world at Thebes."

" And he has been there all the summer ? "

" Yes, fighting the fever like a true knight of
the Red Cross."

" He is a noble fellow ; would it not be better
for you to tell him of our marriage ? "

" No, I can't. I *can't* do it ; and I don't want
him to read it in the papers. You must write
him, and ask him to come."

" O Sara ! "

" Yes, you or Robert ; and I do not think that
monsieur will undertake it."

This with a faint trace of satire in her voice.
She could never quite forgive Feuardent. Margaret looked at her reproachfully, and then said

with a sigh : " You are right ; the letter shall be written to-night."

The writing of the letter was the one painful hour of all that bright, brief courtship. Margaret indited it alone in her room late that night, not without a good deal of feeling ; but the tears were dried and forgotten an hour after, as she fell into a happy dream, soon to be made a reality. The letter was written and despatched, and in due time reached its destination at Thebes. A week passed, and Margaret received no answer, — at which she wondered a little, and then ceased to think about it in the thousand and one busy, happy thoughts that invaded her mind.

The time of the Harvest Home was come, and the whole community in and about Woodbridge was busy in making ready for that joyous festival. The old stone church, where this service had been held for more than a hundred seasons, assumed the appearance of a temple of Ceres. Sheaves of yellow grain stood in the four corners of the sanctuary, and at the chancel-rail lay heaps of rich-toned vegetables, pumpkins shining like new burnished gold, melons of every shape, and great bunches of purple grapes and masses of chrysanthemums flaunting their fringed banners and filling the air with their clean pungent perfume. A vine, heavy with clusters of white grapes, which seemed ready to burst with the sunshine in their hearts, was wreathed across the altar. The delicate stone pillars were outlined with vivid crimson woodbine climbing from base to capital, and the design of the cornice was followed by a garland of ripe ears of corn twisted together, with here and there a branch heavy with apples or pears. At the altar foot lay 'a shining ploughshare, a rake, and a sickle. All these decorations had been planned by Margaret, who had worked with loving willingness to make the temple fair and fitting for that festival, older than Christianity, older than Greece itself, as old as man's gratitude to his Creator for the garnered harvest. Other preparations were making, and from every kitchen of every farm-house in all the country round came the fragrant odors of pumpkin-pies, of pound-cake, of jellies and sweetmeats, of doughnuts, of smoked bacon and sugared hams, of baking beans and roasting meats, for the festival was to be one of good cheer.

The day of the Harvest Home dawned bright and clear, one of those electric autumn days when every breath of the pure bracing air stimulates like a draught of sparkling wine. The sky was one flawless crystal, pale blue at the horizon, and deepening to sapphire at the zenith. There was not a cloud in sight, but about the sun hung a light veil of mist which changed his yellow radiance to a silver light. It was as if the moon had grown as powerful as himself, and, forsaking the realm of night, had sailed boldly into the day and usurped the place of its monarch. The ocean which washes the shores of Woodbridge was not broken by a ripple. It shone like a vast silver shield stretching out to the white horizon.

After the services in the church, where Margaret's fresh sweet voice led the village choir for the last time, the whole congregation poured out upon the church-green, set about with fir-trees, shut in from the high-road by a famous screen of cypress, — the despair and envy of every church and every gardener in the country side. Here were spread long tables laden with the good things the farmers' wives had been so busy in preparing. At the chief of these Margaret presided, cutting with her own hand the first piece from a gigantic game-pie, as wonderful in its flavor and manufacture as the pasty of the Golden Kootoo. The governor of the State — a Ruysdale of the real old-fashioned sort, a florid, handsome old fellow, with the courtly manners of his grandfather's time — stood on Margaret's right hand, the clergyman on her left. In his speech he made a veiled allusion to the event of her marriage, which was received with great enthusiasm. Barrels of fresh cider and kegs of foaming beer were tapped, and healths were drunk and glasses clinked merrily. This last was something of an innovation ; but Margaret had begged to be allowed to contribute to the feast these innocent beverages, as well as the mammoth pasty, the pair of giant turkeys, and the great wedding-cake, big as a small cart-wheel. Robert was introduced to many of the farmers, who had seen Margaret grow up from a 'wee motherless baby to the winsome young woman she now was. They regarded him with a less covert curiosity than her kinsfolk had shown ; and Joseph Halloway, the chief of the selectmen, who had given her apples when she was no higher than his knee, expressed it as his opinion that " Margaret Ruysdale had found a downright smart, handsome-looking husband down South, though he dooes look and talk more like a fur-riner than an American."

It was a joyous day, long remembered at Woodbridge as the merriest Harvest Home there had been in many years. It was held in Margaret's remembrance, all her life through, as a happy day, — the last of her girlhood days ; for on the morrow Robert Feuardent was to claim his bride, and General Ruysdale had pledged his word to deliver over his prisoner to the enemy, even without the return of the hostage heart.

It had come at last, that hour which Robert Feuardent had so ardently desired. The bells of the little church, which was still brave with the triumph of the Harvest, rang out merrily. Bouton de Rose came to the door of his room in the village inn and warned him that the time had come when they should start for the church. He was a pale bridegroom, almost as pale as he had been that day when Margaret had seen him at the Hôtel-Dieu ; but he had never looked handsomer in his life, his bride thought, than at that moment when he turned from the altar and made one involuntary step to meet her as she came up the aisle, all smiles and flowers and blushes, leaning on the General's arm. The bells rang out merrily. The old sexton, who had seen Margaret christened, pulled lustily at the rope, and the air was full of the joyous marriage-peal, echoing from woodland aisle to village street. To Margaret's ears the chime was full of melody ; to Robert it seemed like the silver note of a celestial clarion summoning him to the joy and triumph of his love. To the ears of Sara Harden the bells had a sinister sound. She heard one note, brazen and hoarse as an alarm, swinging through the linked sounds, killing the merriment and turning it to a melancholy minor key. She stood before her mirror, dressed out in all her finery, the prettiest woman — after the bride, who on that day was radiant with that fleeting beauty which comes once in every woman's life — in all the gay throng of guests who had come to witness the wedding of Margaret. She could not shut the doleful sound out from her ears, though she tried bravely, as with blanched face she turned away from the glass that a moment before had shown so rosy and smiling a reflection.

"Are you ready, my dear?" asked her husband.

"Yes."

"How pale you look! Are you not well?"

"Yes, yes, Gaffer; it is nothing. Bring my smelling-salts."

Her hand was on the door, when again the chime rang out, and again she heard that note of grief swelling now like a dirge, and sending the blood tingling through her veins. She gave a terrified cry, and mindless of her laces and bravery, fell upon her knees. In a moment her husband had her in his arms, trying to soothe the unaccountable paroxysm that shook her frame. It passed quickly, and she was soon quietly weeping upon his shoulder.

"Go, dear; go, my good, kind husband, and leave me. I *cannot* go to that wedding. I shall never be missed; and if I should be, say that I am ill!"

"I can't leave you, Sara; I never saw you so upset before."

"You *must* go, dear, dear Darius; but come back soon, for I don't know, indeed, what ails me. I am afraid to be alone with my thoughts, they are so strange and terrible."

She *was* missed at the church by many; most of all by the susceptible young Ruysdale, on whose heart her perfections had made a very deep impression. They came in search of her when the bridal party returned to the house; and yielding to their solicitation, Sara Harden touched her pale cheeks with a little rouge—for perhaps the second time in her life—and joined the festivities below. Her usual vivacious spirits were missing, however,—which did not prevent the feast from being a merry one; for confiding her depression to the favored cousin, she passed the time with him in a remote corner of the conservatory, where the casual observer supposed them to be carrying on a desperate flirtation. Here Bouton de Rose came in search of her, and here he did brave and valiant battle with the cousin for possession of the seat by the little lady's side. But the impressionable Ruysdale was immovable; and until the moment came when all gathered together to say farewell to the bride, they remained in the shadow of the palms.

"Good-by, good-by, my Atalanta!" Sara whispered, as her turn came to take Margaret in her arms in an affectionate embrace; and Margaret felt that the cheek laid for a moment against her own was wet with tears. They were the only ones that marred the smiles of that bright wedding-day, and they were forgotten five minutes after they were dry.

Amidst a storm of rice and satin shoes, of kisses and farewells, Robert and Margaret left the old Ruysdale mansion and started on that first and shortest stage of their life-journey.

. . . .

The summer was past, and Thebes, the broken and desolate city, was beginning to give thanks for her deliverance from the pestilence. In the churches thanksgivings were offered, and in the decimated households men and women were rejoicing for the lives of the dear ones who had been spared to them. At the headquarters of the Aid Society, whose members had ministered so nobly and generously to the suffering community, no medicines were given out now, no orders for the grim appliances of burial, but strong soup and jellies for the convalescents, cordials and tonics for those who were still weak. The nurses and doctors, such of them as had been spared, were taking their departure, bearing away with them the thanks and blessing of the people unto whose cry they had hearkened. Business began to be resumed, and men and women met in the streets and market-place without that dread avoidance of contagion which has separated each man from his brothers. A hearty willingness to lend a hand to those who had suffered most was noticeable, even in those professions wherein envy and jealousy are thought to be the only binding links A thoughtful cheerfulness was the prevailing expression of men's faces ; the most frivolous among them was chastened by what he had endured, the most austere softened by the sorrow of the past summer. In the columns of the local press the bulletin of deaths had resumed its normal dimensions, and the marriage notices, which had ceased entirely, began to come slowly into the office. The streets lost their desolate emptiness and the houses assumed their ordinary appearance.

The vengeance of the pauper had been wreaked upon the rich man, and the pestilence was dead, or slept, glutted with its victims. It is as sure as that thunder-clap shall follow lightning-flash that the neglected and squalid denizens of the vile tenements shall breed in their misery and filth a disease which when it has grown strong is not to be stifled in the quarter whence it sprang, but will walk abroad and will not be denied at the doors of the grand houses where the beggar dares not ask for bread. The cities of the world have suffered many such a chastening as that which Thebes has endured. May they profit by the warning and follow the example of the people of that city, who, when their sick were whole again, tarried not, but purged and cleansed the town, wherein will never again be found foot-hold for the dreaded visitor !

It was a time of rest and thanksgiving in all the city, with one exception : the house of Madame Anna wore the darkened look which betokens the presence of illness. The blinds were drawn, the street outside was strewn with straw, and the heavy knocker muffled. Day and night Hero sat beside the door, that no visitor should disturb the sufferer who lay in the long dining-room, the largest and airiest apartment in the house. The callers were not a few; hardly a quarter of an hour passed without some anxious inquiry, to which Hero would answer with a mournful shake of the head, —

" No better."

For the time of the fever was past, and the illness which laid Philip Rondelet low bore no trace of the baneful disease he had fought so bravely. Men and women had time to turn from their own cares and ask news of him who had won the love and gratitude of the community.

" No better."

The grievous response came slowly, with a monotonous reiteration which tortured Therese when it fell from the lips of physicians who tended him with unfailing devotion. Their chief had been stricken down ; the man who had inspired them with faith and courage in the never-to-be-forgotten weeks now lay ill of an insidious disease whose nature they could not determine, whose progress they failed to stay.

From the hour when he had been first attacked, — it was soon after he had received a number of letters, Therese remembered, — she had hardly left him. She took such rest and refreshment as were necessary at the farther corner of the lofty room, whose gay appointments were strangely out of keeping with the scene to which they afforded a background. Certain of the pictures which she deemed unfit for dying eyes she banished, and above the bed she hung a crucifix, the parting gift of the Abbess who had been as a mother to her. It was a wonderful work of art, carven of flawless ivory, mellow with the centuries which had passed since the master-hand which wrought it had crumbled to dust. The ebony cross brought sharply into relief the emaciated body and the beautiful grieved face. Philip had told Therese that she possessed a treasure in this bit of carving, and she hung it where his eyes could linger on the wondrous apotheosis of pain.

One morning, perhaps ten days after he had succumbed to the illness developed by the almost superhuman toil of the summer, Therese, finding her patient apparently much improved, left him in charge of one of the physicians and went out to take a brief walk. She was gone only a short time, but when she returned she found Hero waiting for her at the gate.

Philip had been asking for her. With a feeling as if her whole life had paused for a moment, she trembled and leaned against the black creature for support; then the weakness was conquered, and she entered the house. At the threshold of the sick room she was met by the grave face of the doctor. "It is all over," he said gently. "Come and see how quietly he died, — without a pang or a struggle."

He led her to the bedside. Therese looked at him for a moment, and then, kneeling beside him, whispered :

"Look! it is the face of the dead Christ of the crucifix!"

Even as the stigmata appeared of old on the body of St. Francis, so was the shadow of that face reflected on the dead face of Philip Rondelet, a weak and sinful man, who had given his life to save his fellow-men.

In the great concourse of people that followed all that was mortal of Philip Rondelet to the grave, all distinctions of class and sect were swept away, as they never fail to be in times of deep feeling. Roman priest and Jewish rabbi, the noisy atheistical preacher and the rigid Presbyterian divine, walked together behind the two chief mourners, — his foster-brother and servant Hero, and Therese, the woman whom he had saved from death. Only these two, out of all the friends who had known and admired him before he had joined the forsaken garrison at Thebes! The bells of the churches tolled as the procession wound through the streets, their harsh iron clangor, echoing from belfry to belfry, resounding in the aisles of the silent city of the dead, toward which the crowd was moving. It may be that their deep, hoarse notes were wafted even farther, and that they blended faintly with the marriage-chimes with which the Woodbridge woods were so merry that day. It may be that to one sensitive ear the mournful echo of a dirge was audible above the wedding-bells, and that the tears of Hero and Therese were not the only ones shed that day for Philip Rondelet.

FINIS.